The Internet and Social

Ideal for use as a core or secondary text in lower division social inequalities or social problems courses, this book explains how the changing nature and uses of the Internet not only mirror today's social inequalities, but are also at the heart of how stratification is now taking place. A pioneering work, both intellectually and pedagogically.

James C. Witte (Ph.D., Harvard University) is Professor of Sociology and Director of the Center for Social Science Research at George Mason University. Witte was previously Chair of the Communication and Information Technology section of the American Sociological Association.

Susan E. Mannon (Ph.D., University of Wisconsin-Madison) is an Adjunct Professor of Sociology at Utah State University. She teaches and does research in the areas of Social Inequality and International Development. Her work has appeared in *Gender & Society*, *Human Organization*, and *Sociological Spectrum*.

Contemporary Sociological Perspectives

Edited by **Valerie Jenness**, University of California, Irvine
and **Jodi O'Brien**, Seattle University

This innovative series is for all readers interested in books that provide frameworks for making sense of the complexities of contemporary social life. Each of the books in this series uses a sociological lens to provide current critical and analytical perspectives on significant social issues, patterns, and trends. The series consists of books that integrate the best ideas in sociological thought with an aim toward public education and engagement. These books are designed for use in the classroom as well as for scholars and socially curious general readers.

Published:
Political Justice and Religious Values by Charles F. Andrain
GIS and Spatial Analysis for the Social Sciences by Robert Nash Parker
and Emily K. Asencio
Hoop Dreams on Wheels: Disability and the Competitive Wheelchair Athlete
by Ronald J. Berger
Violence Against Women by Douglas Brownridge
Media and Middle Class Moms by Lara Descartes and Conrad Kottak
Watching T.V. Is Not Required by Bernard McGrane and John Gunderson

Forthcoming:
Social Statistics: The Basics and Beyond by Thomas J. Linneman
Gender Circuits: The Evolution of Bodies and Identities in a Technological Age
by Eve Shapiro
The State of Sex: Tourism, Sex and Sin in the New American Heartland by Barbara Brents,
Crystal Jackson, and Kathryn Hausbeck
Sociological Storytelling: Reflections on the Research Experience by Sarah Fenstermaker
and Nikki Jones

Also of Interest from Routledge:
Understanding Society through Popular Music by Joe Kotarba and Phillip Vannini
Foodies: Democracy and Distinction in the Gourmet Foodscape by Josée Johnston
and Shyon Baumann
Global Gender Research: Transnational Perspectives edited by Christine Bose
and Minjeong Kim
Making Transnational Feminism: Rural Women, NGO Activists, and Northern Donors in Brazil by Millie Thayer
Operation Gatekeeper and Beyond: The War on Illegals and the Remaking of the U.S. – Mexico Boundary by Joseph Nevins
Poverty Capital: Microfinance and the Making of Development by Ananya Roy
Regression Analysis for the Social Sciences by Rachel A. Gordon

The Internet and Social Inequalities

James C. Witte
George Mason University

Susan E. Mannon
Utah State University

Routledge
Taylor & Francis Group

NEW YORK AND LONDON

First published 2010
by Routledge
270 Madison Avenue, New York, NY 10016

Simultaneously published in the UK
by Routledge
2 Park Square, Milton Park, Abingdon, Oxon OX14 4RN

Routledge is an imprint of the Taylor & Francis Group, an informa business

© 2010 Taylor & Francis

Typeset in Adobe Caslon and Copperplate Gothic by
RefineCatch Limited, Bungay, Suffolk
Printed and bound in the United States of America on acid-free paper by
Edwards Brothers, Inc.

Library of Congress Cataloging in Publication Data
Witte, James C.
The internet and social inequalities / James C. Witte, Susan E.
Mannon—1st ed.
p. cm.—(Contemporary sociological perspectives)
Includes bibliographical references and index.
1. Internet—Social aspects.   2. Technological innovations—Social
aspects.   3. Social networks.   I. Mannon, Susan E.   II. Title.
HM851.W58   2010
303.48'33—dc22
2009028020

ISBN10: 0–415–96320–6 (hbk)
ISBN10: 0–415–96319–2 (pbk)
ISBN10: 0–203–86163–9 (ebk)

ISBN13: 978–0–415–96320–6 (hbk)
ISBN13: 978–0–415–96319–0 (pbk)
ISBN13: 978–0–203–86163–9 (ebk)

TABLE OF CONTENTS

SERIES FOREWORD

This innovative series is for all readers interested in books that provide frameworks for making sense of the complexities of contemporary social life. Each of the books in this series uses a sociological lens to provide current critical and analytical perspectives on significant social issues, patterns, and trends. The series consists of books that integrate the best ideas in sociological thought with an aim toward public education and engagement. These books are designed for use in the classroom as well as for scholars and socially curious general readers.

The Internet and Social Inequalities moves well beyond the discussion encapsulated by the concept "the digital divide," and broadens and deepens concern about the Internet as evolving technology that is inextricably intertwined with—and ultimately consequential for—inequality. In this book, Witte and Mannon remind us that when using the Internet, "you're not simply typing and clicking; you're participating in a social world in which patterns of inclusion and exclusion may be observed." With this in mind, this book provides a fresh view of the Internet by interrogating this social world empirically and theoretically. Drawing on a variety of compelling data sets, Witte and Mannon paint a systematic and multi-faceted empirical picture of patterns of Internet use that speaks clearly and forcefully to how Internet use is organized around social statuses, especially race, class, gender, education level, occupational attainment, and age. By positioning Internet use as both a social institution and a social structure, they subject empirical patterns of Internet use to three of the most well-known sociological frame-works: a conflict perspective, a cultural perspective, and a functionalist perspective. By doing so, they take the reader on an enlightening journey that simultaneously provides vivid examples of the utility of social theory and illuminates dynamics underlying differences in Internet use as well as how we (differentially) benefit from being online. By taking this journey, readers learn about the sociological real-ities of Internet use and inequality, including how the Internet serves to exacerbate existing social inequalities; they also gain an appreciation for how technology can—and at some historical moments does—draw upon, transform, institutionalize, and further seemingly intractable social structures of inequality. By the end of the journey, readers are aware that "the digital divide" is not only about access to technology; increasingly important is that it's also about the plethora of ways we use technology and the consequences of that use. Finally, *The Internet and Social Inequalities* will impress upon researchers, policy makers, students, and the general public that we should be concerned with inequalities that manifest *among* the population of Internet users, paying particular attention to the unforeseen consequences born of the growth in Internet use and the changes in the content of the Internet.

Valerie Jenness and Jodi O'Brien
Series Editors

PREFACE AND ACKNOWLEDGMENTS

The disparities in Internet access in the United States and beyond have sparked much debate in the popular press about the "digital divide." The discipline of sociology has been slow to contribute to this debate, which is surprising given that sociology has a long tradition in the study of social inequality. This book takes social theories developed by sociology's "founding fathers"—Karl Marx, Max Weber, and Emile Durkheim—and applies them to the question of Internet inequality. Because this book is grounded in these core perspectives on inequality, it provides a clear and concise illustration of sociology's theoretical landscape. Moreover, the book fills a major gap in the sociological study of social inequality by applying these theories to a critical social problem of our day.

Marx, Weber, Durkheim, and other early sociologists developed the theoretical foundations of sociology in response to the social changes associated with the Industrial Revolution. Today, we are in the midst of an information and technological revolution that compels us to revisit some of these early social theories. A few exceptions notwithstanding, mainstream sociology has given little attention to the impact of the Internet at the individual and societal levels. If the reaction to the Industrial Revolution had been the same, one could ask whether the discipline of sociology would even exist today. With this book, we hope to show that sociology has much to offer in understanding inequality in the information age.

Despite the Internet's global reach, we focus on U.S. society. This focus is not meant to overlook the depth of the international digital divide, but simply to bound the analysis. Similarly, most of the discussion in this book is concentrated on the years between 1995 and 2007, despite the significance of earlier eras of technological change and the importance of future trends in Internet use. It is within these geographical and historical brackets that we engage the theoretical perspectives of sociology to show how they can help us understand the link between the Internet and inequality.

This book is organized as follows. In Chapter 2, we provide a descriptive view of the digital divide in the United States during the time in question. Chapters 3 through 5 are the main empirical chapters of the book and each uses one of the three theoretical approaches to inequality to understand a different aspect of the Internet. In these chapters, we draw primarily on data from the Pew Internet & American Life Project, which conducts an ongoing series of surveys on Internet use of a nationally representative sample of Americans. Chapter 6 takes a view toward the future, knowing that the future comes at us very quickly in the realm of technology. Today's Internet will not be tomorrow's communication and information technology. On the other hand, a communication and information infrastructure of some form is not likely to go away anytime soon.

Advice and encouragement for this project came from many sources. First, we thank Steve Rutter, Social Sciences and Sociology Publisher at Routledge, for his support and for his patience. Research support related to this project was provided by Kevin Foster, Abhijith Holehonnur, Xue Liu, and Jennifer Turchi. Comments on draft chapters of the book were provided by Thomas Allen, Mary Fairbairn, Tracie Gesel, Kelly Linker, Thomas Linneman, Catherine Mobley, Constance Witte, Allison Hurst, Vincent Serravallo, Linda Benbow, Laura Robinson, and Gerhard Fuchs.

1

A Sociology of the Internet

Although it has several other properties that have institutional consequences, on the whole the Internet is loosely coupled to the institutional world around it. It does not inherently promote freedom or oppression, hierarchy or decentralization, privacy or social control, individualist or collectivist values, markets or socialism. Considered narrowly as a technology, it is capable of participating in any combination of social orders. Considered more broadly as a malleable architecture interacting with a complex and contested institutional environment, however, the Internet is a complicated phenomenon indeed.

—*Agre* 2002

Introduction

For many young people today, it's hard to imagine a time before the Internet, harder still to imagine a time when people relied on typewriters and whiteout. But consider these statistics. As late as 1994, only 11 percent of American households had access to the Internet (NTIA 1995). By 2007, that statistic was well over 60 percent.[1] And this was just the figure for *household* Internet access; well over 70 percent of American households had someone who had access to the Internet at some location. In the span of just one decade, the Internet had entered our homes, our schools, and our workplaces—not to mention our libraries, our cafes, and our cell phones—to become a major feature of daily life. Given the rapid spread of Internet technology, it's easy to see why the Internet might be celebrated for bringing about a social transformation in American life.

But has the Internet really brought about such a profound transformation? Even in the early days of the Internet, many suspected that information technology was mirroring rather than transforming social divides in the United States. Researchers pointed to a racial divide (Hoffman and Novak 1998) for example, and a rural–urban divide (Strover 1999) in Internet access. Policy makers and social scientists even began to speak of a "digital divide," or a divide between those who had access to the Internet and those who, due to lack of opportunity or interest, remained offline (NTIA 1998, 1999). More recent research suggests that new "digital divides" are emerging, as Internet technology evolves and certain groups become more sophisticated at navigating the web (DiMaggio et al. 2001). And some scholars argue that we need to move beyond a singular concern over Internet *access* to tackle differences in Internet skills and behavior as they manifest among Internet users. As DiMaggio et al. (2001, p. 52) argue: "Now that more than half of Americans now go online, we should pursue a more differentiated approach to understanding the Internet's implications for social and economic inequality – one that focuses upon the extent and causes of different returns to Internet use for different kinds of users." Hargittai (2006), for example, points out that spelling mistakes limit the ability of the less educated to take advantage of online search engines, a limitation that is compounded for some by an inability to read and comprehend materials once they find them.

DiMaggio et al. (2001) raise the importance of looking sociologically at these digital divides. Specifically, they point to social inequalities that linger long after the headlines about the Internet's revolutionary potential. These inequalities are no small matter. As political participation moves online, newspapers and books evolve into digital formats, social networking occurs through web applications, and e-commerce expands, participation in public life necessitates some Internet access and competency. Those without an email address or a Facebook profile may become excluded from the larger society. Internet access and use, then, are not simply mapped onto existing inequalities; they may exacerbate them over time as offline groups become marginalized from the Internet and from popular forms of political, social, and economic participation. In its current form, then, the Internet is a paradox of twenty-first century American life, at once an emblem of a free and open society and an active reproducer and possible accelerator of social inequality.

The purpose of this book is to explore this paradox by moving beyond inequalities in Internet access to explore differences in how we use the Internet and how we benefit from being online. Its relevance to you, the reader, is real. Think of all the things you do (or don't do) online every day, the information you have access to, the people you interact with, the products you buy, and the words you share. You're not simply typing and clicking; you're participating in a social world in which patterns of inclusion and exclusion may be observed. These patterns are of interest to sociologists, who study how individuals interact in the context of larger social structures. The norms and rules that govern social interaction do not stop when we go online, although they might be transformed. The Internet can and *should* be studied from a sociological perspective because it is fundamentally a social institution. Who has enjoyed access to the Internet? And how does this access combine with variables like income and education to turn a profit, consolidate power, and mark status? Finally, how do these patterns exclude segments of the population from the social, political, and economic potential of the Internet? These are the questions that we'll explore throughout this book. First, however, let's explore further the research on the "digital divide" and the history of this divide.

The Digital Divide

No one denies that the Internet and related forms of communication and information technology have had a profound effect on American society and beyond. Yet, as we've mentioned, an increasing number of people now acknowledge a "digital divide." By the late 1990s, policy makers and researchers noticed that the digital revolution was leaving many groups behind. The 1999 United Nations *Human Development*

Report, for example, observed the following about Internet use worldwide:

> The typical Internet user worldwide is male, under 35 years old, with a college education and high income, urban-based and English-speaking—a member of a very elite minority worldwide. The consequence? The network society is creating parallel communications systems: one for those with income, education and—literally—connections, giving plentiful information at low cost and high speed; the other for those without connections, blocked by high barriers of time, cost and uncertainty and dependent on outdated information. With people in these two systems living and competing side by side, the advantages of connection are overpowering. The voices and concerns of people already living in human poverty—lacking incomes, education and access to public institutions—are being increasingly marginalized. (UN 1999, p. 63)

This observation gets to the heart of what social scientists call the "digital divide," or the gap between those with access to the Internet and those without.

Because inequalities in Internet access have such far-reaching consequences, working toward universal access has been a major concern of policy makers. In the United States, for example, the National Telecommunications and Information Administration (NTIA) has tracked Internet access and developed policy recommendations to close gaps in such access (NTIA 1995, 1998, 1999, 2000, 2002). Among the "digital divides" noted by the NTIA is a divide between urban and rural areas, between whites and non-whites, between the young and old, and between the economically active and inactive (see DiMaggio et al. 2001 for a review). The NTIA and the literature more generally tends to frame this discussion in terms of haves and have nots. Either you have Internet access at home, work, or school or you do *not* have Internet access. Although it is certainly important to study differences in Internet access, there are also important differences in Internet use among those who enjoy some form of access. Perhaps an individual has Internet access at home, but their dial-up speed is slow and hence their Internet usage is limited. Perhaps an individual has high-speed Internet, but little knowledge of search engines and how to "surf" the Internet, narrowing the scope of what they can get out of being online. The research and policy agenda must be broad enough to tackle these differences and the inequalities they produce.

Given the complexities in Internet inequality, this study approaches the digital divide differently from bodies like the NTIA. It shows how Internet inequalities are manifesting among the online population and the overall population. In doing so, it builds on recent research suggesting that there is something more to the "digital divide" than simply access. Scholars have discovered differences in Internet use that include variations in connection speed (Kling 1998), where individuals access the Internet (Bimber 2000), what technical and cognitive skills they bring to bear in navigating the Internet (Hargittai 2002), the length of time they spend online (Bonfadelli 2002), and the purpose for which they use the Internet (Spooner and Rainey 2000). In this book, we'll consider differences in how frequently people go online, what activities they do online, and what they get out of their online experience. We hypothesize that these differences map onto existing inequalities in American society, with historically disadvantaged groups going online with less frequency, for less productive purposes, and for a smaller social and financial return. We also suggest that these differences could exacerbate existing inequalities, such that privileged social groups consolidate their power and heighten their privileged status through the use of the Internet.

In addition to building on a critical area of research, we'll tell this story through the lens of some classic sociological perspectives: the conflict perspective, the cultural perspective, and the functionalist perspective. Each perspective provides a provocative explanation for how and why Internet inequalities exist. Using recent data on Internet use in American society, we'll test some of these ideas empirically to determine their explanatory power. After reading this book, you'll have a sense of the variety of ways that sociologists can examine the Internet as a social institution and social structure, not to mention a greater appreciation for what differences in Internet use might mean for social inequality.

DiMaggio et al. (2001) contend that inequalities embedded in Internet technology are not due to the technology itself, but to the ways in which that technology has developed over time. Thus, before we embark on this theoretical and empirical treatment of the Internet, a brief history of the Internet is in order. We'll use a novel source of data to explore this history. Internationally, two groups are largely responsible for developing and coordinating Internet standards and protocols: the Internet Engineering Task Force (IETF) and the Internet Architecture Board (IAB). Both groups are part of the international non-profit organization known as the Internet Society and both have published a series of "Requests for Comment" (RFCs).[2] Numbered 1 through 5242, the RFC series documents the development of the principles of network computing, including the TCP/IP communication protocols that are the technical backbone of today's Internet.[3] In addition to their technical content, the RFCs offer unique insights into how individuals and groups contested and negotiated the principles of the Internet, its organizational structure, and its major design features.[4] This discussion will provide some context and background for the analytic chapters that follow.

The Advent of Network Computing

The purpose of the early Internet was to provide a means of communication for U.S. political and military leaders in the event of nuclear war. Baffled by the task of securing a central network facility against enemy missiles, staff researchers at the RAND Corporation proposed a novel solution in the early 1960s: create a communications network that could bypass a central command structure. The idea was to put in place a communications infrastructure that had no central authority, such that it could operate and remain intact even after command structures were destroyed during wartime. At first glance an elegant and creative solution, such a network required enormous technical development. Beginning in the fall of 1969, the U.S. Defense Advanced Research

Projects Agency (DARPA) funded a team to build computer network nodes.

While one group of young Americans was fighting in the jungles of Vietnam and another was marching in the streets, a third group was preparing to build a computer network that would transform American society. In August of 1969, the first node was created at the University of California-Los Angeles (UCLA). Three additional nodes were added later that fall at Stanford, the University of California-Santa Barbara and the University of Utah. A core group of network developers, primarily graduate students in computer science, operated out of the Network Measurement Center at UCLA. This group shared an intellectual outlook that closely mirrored the network that they would build—a decentralized, iconoclastic, can-do sensibility that did not take itself too seriously. Writing 30 years later, Steve Crocker, a pioneer of network computing, explains:

> We were frankly too scared to imagine that we could define an all-inclusive set of protocols that would serve indefinitely. We envisioned a continual process of evolution and addition, and obviously this is what's happened. The RFCs themselves also represented a certain sense of fear . . . . Mindful that our group was informal, junior and unchartered, I wanted to emphasize these notes were the beginning of a dialog and not an assertion of control. (RFC #255)

Despite the hesitancy and humility with which this group of junior scholars approached the development of the Internet, the technical skeleton that they would construct would serve as the foundation upon which our online world was built.

Though the Internet was born in a loosely organized environment, it did not take long for an organizational structure to emerge. For example, RFC#140, issued in 1971, sets out to organize and manage a growing group of scientists and research centers involved in the Internet's construction. The need for some structure was understandable; between 1969 and 1971, the number of participating scientists

grew from nine to 60 (RFC#10; RFC#155).[5] An organizational structure emerged, but a strong emphasis on the ethos of science remained.
RFC#1025, for instance, describes procedures for a series of "bake-
offs," which were venues for scientists to present and advocate different
designs and communications protocols. At these venues, most of which
occurred in the 1970s and 1980s, competing designs were evaluated
and discussed in collaborative fashion. As these two examples suggest,
there was an ongoing tension between an ethos of science, which
stressed open collaboration, and a bureaucratic personality, which
stressed formal hierarchy, throughout the early years of the Internet.

In 1981, the BITNET (or the "Because It's Time NETwork," also
known as the "Because It's There NETwork") was started as a cooperative network at the City University of New York. The BITNET
provided electronic mail and listserv servers to distribute information,
as well as file transfer technology. Within just one year, this network
spanned the United States and the Atlantic, connecting to its European
counterpart EARN (European Academic and Research Network).
BITNET was an academic network and it facilitated communication
in the name of research and education. As a cooperative network,
participating organizations and universities contributed communication lines, temporary data storage, and the processing power necessary
for the network to function. At its peak in 1992, the BITNET
consisted of approximately 1,400 organizations in 49 countries.

Developing at the same time as BITNET, the Internet offered a
network architecture that was considerably more open. The Internet
was also well suited to the introduction of the personal computer and
local area networks (LANs), or networks of computers in relative prox-
imity to one another, which became popularized in the second half of
the 1980s. In many ways, the pivotal event in the Internet's ascendancy
over BITNET came in 1991, with the introduction of the "Gopher"
Internet search engine at the University of Minnesota. RFC#1436
introduced "Gopher" to the Internet community:

> **gopher** n. 1. Any of various short tailed, burrowing mammals of
> the family *Geomyidae*, of North America. 2. (Amer. colloq.) Native

or inhabitant of Minnesota: the Gopher State. 3. (Amer. colloq.) One who runs errands, does odd-jobs, fetches or delivers documents for office staff. 4. (computer tech.) Software following a simple protocol for tunneling through a TCP/IP Internet.

The introduction of Gopher and other Internet search engines significantly altered the way that the user community—still primarily scientists and researchers—began to use the Internet. A rapidly growing Internet made available online not simply text files, but program codes and other forms of information. Search engines provided the means to catalogue and explore the growing volume of information. Programs to transfer information (e.g., FTP) put information on the desktops of scholars almost instantly.

In late 1990, a computer scientist at the European Organization for Nuclear Research (CERN) invented the World Wide Web (WWW), which transformed the Internet into the user-friendly graphic user interface that most people are familiar with today. CERN is an international organization that builds and operates research facilities for particle physicists. Most researchers spend some time at the CERN site, but typically they work at universities and laboratories in their home countries. Given this environment, the WWW served not only as a vehicle for exchanging information, but also as a tool to encourage active collaboration within the CERN community. The WWW used "hyperlinks," which provided point-and-click access rather than typed and complex commands. Hyperlinking adhered to the foundational characteristics of network computing—democratic, decentralized, and decidedly nonlinear. There was no hierarchy, with any site capable of referencing any other site. There was no central command, with responsibility for content and access resting with owners of the site. And there was no single path from point A to point B, with various pathways through the Internet available.

Another critical event in Internet technology occurred in 1993, when Marc Andreessen and a team of students and staff at the University of Illinois developed Mosaic, one of the first web browsers. As a web browser, Mosaic opened access to the WWW by making web pages available to anyone with a personal computer, not just scientists at supercomputing centers or research labs with serious computational power. A year later, Andreessen founded Netscape Communications Corporation, and the company began to develop the Netscape Navigator web browser, which brought the Internet into homes and businesses around the world.

Evolution of the Internet

Within a short period of time, then, the public enjoyed access to this growing web of information known as the Internet. Ed Krol, who would later write the first popular guide to the Internet, *The Whole Internet: User's Guide and Catalog* (1992), authored RFC#1118 in 1989. Entitled "The Hitchhiker's Guide to the Internet," this memo noted and attended to the growing number of new users. And beginning with RFC#1150, issued in March of 1990, the network working group initiated a new sub-series of RFCs called FYIs (For Your Information), which were intended for a wide audience. By November of the same year, the Internet development community began speaking of the commercialization of the Internet (RFC#1192), making it abundantly clear that a new day was dawning. In a 1993 FYI, Krol observed:

> Businesses are now discovering that running multiple networks is expensive. Some are beginning to look to the Internet for "one-stop" network shopping. They were scared away in the past by policies which excluded or restricted commercial use. Many of these policies are under review and will change. As these restrictions drop, commercial use of the Internet will become progressively more common. (RFC#1462)

By the early 1990s, developers were considering ways to deliver new Internet services, "including teleconferencing, remote seminars, tele-science, and distributed simulation" (RFC#1633). And by 1996, an Internet standard for the encoding of audio and video data had been released (RFC#1890) and work was beginning on GPS-based addressing and routing (RFC#2009).

An interesting marker of the changing character of the Internet came in 1993, when RFC#1550 solicited white papers on design requirements for the next generation of Internet protocols (IPng). For our purposes, who responded to the solicitation and the topics they addressed are of interest. Responses included developing protocols for determining market viability (RFC#1669), developing a cellular industry (RFC#1674), constructing large corporate networks (RFC#1678), and nurturing other commercial ventures (RFC#1672; RFC#1686). Clearly the Internet was no longer just about science. If we were to designate one moment as emblematic of the commercial transformation of the Internet, it would have to be February 1996, which saw the publication of RFC#1898, "CyberCash Credit Card Protocol Version 0.8." In this document, Crocker explained:

> CyberCash, Inc. of Reston, Virginia was founded in August of 1994 to partner with financial institutions and providers of goods and services to deliver a safe, convenient and inexpensive system for making payments on the Internet . . . . CyberCash serves as a conduit through which payments can be transported quickly, easily and safely between buyers, sellers and their banks. Significantly—much as it is the real world of commerce—the buyer and seller need not have any prior existing relationship. As a neutral third party whose sole concern is ensuring the delivery of payments from one party to another, CyberCash is the linchpin in delivering spontaneous consumer electronic commerce on the Internet.[6]

In 1999, RFC #2706 provided a set of guidelines for web merchants to use, which facilitated web-based shopping for consumers. The era of e-commerce had arrived.

As commercial aspects to the Internet evolved in the 1990s, Internet applications were also evolving. To many observers, the Internet was reinvented with the development of so-called Web2.0 sites. Tim O'Reilly, a prominent publisher of computer books, first coined the term "Web2.0." In a 2005 article called "What is Web2.0," he compares

Netscape and Google to help distinguish Web2.0 from its predecessor, Web1.0. Whereas Netscape (representing Web1.0) acted as a web browser, with a "webtop" replacing a desktop, Google (representing Web2.0) is neither a server nor a browser. As O'Reilly explains: "Much like a phone call, which happens not just on the phones at either end of the call, but on the network in between, Google happens in the space between browser and search engine and destination content server, as an enabler or middleman between the user and his or her online experience." Google, according to O'Reilly, had "none of the trappings of the old software industry." Indeed, there was no software packaged and sold. It was simply "delivered as a service" to Internet users.

Web2.0, according to O'Reilly, is a platform not an application. It brings an end to the software release cycle through web services that are being continually updated on the server side. Thus, none of the emblematic Web2.0 sites requires the user to download software. Instead, they offer users the chance to be members of the site. Site members provide information directly through user profiles or indirectly through logs of online behavior that allow continual updating and customization of the site. Although Web2.0 sites do not require a software download, many of them offer desktop tools as free downloads. These tools typically enhance the site's performance or enable a "mashup" with another Web2.0 site. The idea is to share selected data across sites in ways that add value to the originating application. Looking at Web2.0 applications, and increasingly across the web, all but the smallest of sites are moving from static pages to dynamic designs. This shift in design allows web content to be easily added, edited, and maintained by "content managers" rather than "html programmers."

Most readers will know Google, Wikipedia, eBay, and Amazon as the icons of Web2.0. (For a list of specific Web2.0 sites and their Web1.0 equivalents, see Figure 1.1.) To capture the defining features of Web2.0, though, let's review a less universally known site: Digg.com. To get a full sense of this Web2.0 example, you should go online and click through the site, although a sample page is provided in Figure 1.2.

Web1.0		Web2.0
DoubleClick	⟶	Google AdSense
Ofoto	⟶	Flickr
Akamai	⟶	BitTorrent
mp3.com	⟶	Napster
Britannica Online	⟶	Wikipedia
personal websites	⟶	blogging
evite	⟶	upcoming.org and EVDB
domain name speculation	⟶	search engine optimization
page views	⟶	cost per click
screen scraping	⟶	web services
publishing	⟶	participation
content management systems	⟶	Wikis
directories (taxonomy)	⟶	tagging ("folksonomy")
stickiness	⟶	syndication

Figure 1.1 Differences in Web1.0 and Web2.0 (source: O'Reilly, Tim, "What is Web2.0," www.oreillynet.com/pub/a/oreilly/tim/news/2005/09/03/what-is-web-20.htm).

As you do this and as you read the following discussion of Digg.com, keep in mind O'Reilly's list of defining characteristics of Web2.0:

1 it is a platform not an application;
2 it harnesses collective intelligence;
3 it is data-driven and database management is the requisite core competency;
4 it brings an end to the software release cycle through web services that are continually updated on the server side;
5 its goal is simple, lightweight programming;
6 it creates software for multiple devices with a move from the PC as the default platform; and
7 it strives for a dynamic, multi-media user experience.

Digg.com is a site that allows individuals to share information from elsewhere on the web. Individuals provide links to images, articles, videos, and so on, and the Digg community vote on, or Digg, what pieces they like best. The items with the most popular votes, or Diggs, are showcased front and center at the Digg.com site. On a random

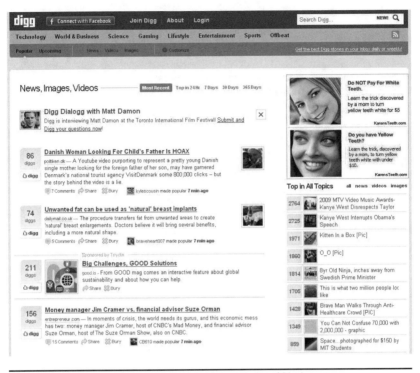

Figure 1.2 The Digg.com home page (reprinted by permission of Digg).

winter day in 2009, the top items on Digg.com included a story about how the religious right views stem cell research and a video of someone using a fart machine at a city council meeting! Many other websites even offer "Digg it" buttons at the end of their articles to encourage readers to share the information with the Digg community. Desktop widgets—virtual tools placed on desktops that provide services such as showing the current time and weather—allow users to vote for an item on Digg without actually going to Digg. Web applications and "mashups" provide a similar service. For example, an application can be loaded onto a Facebook profile that enables friends to see stories that an individual most recently Dugg.

Digg.com embodies collective intelligence, a defining feature of Web2.0, in that it acts as a clearinghouse for what Digg users find of interest. As for the ownership of "contributed content" the terms of use agreement for Digg is very clear and typical:

> By uploading, submitting or otherwise disclosing or distributing Content for display or inclusion on the Site, you represent and warrant that you own all rights in the Content and you agree that the Content will be dedicated to the public domain under the Creative Commons Public Domain Dedication, available at http://creativecommons.org/licenses/publicdomain.

In other words, by posting a comment you give up ownership of the comment as intellectual property. The actual stories, however, are a different matter. Digg does not host any of the content that is featured on the site. Rather, for each story, the Digg database holds a link to the location where the story is available. When a story attracts considerable attention, the original host may crash due to an increase in traffic sent to that site from Digg, known as the "Digg effect" or being "Dugg to death."

As is typical of Web2.0 applications, Digg.com has frequently tested out new features and enhanced its site. Digg started as a website with only text and no graphics or advertisements. It is now in its third major iteration. There is no software release cycle. Instead, new features are added when needed. For example, when a large number of pictures began to be posted on the site, Digg implemented a picture section to make it easier to search and sort posts by media type. Due to the increasing number of mobile Internet users, Digg also launched m.digg.com, a version of Digg designed for Blackberries, iPhones, and other technology appliances. Figure 1.3 showcases an m.digg page, illustrating the way in which Web2.0 moves beyond the desktop computer platform and the traditional web page experience. Light on graphics, the mobile page retrieves the same data as the standard site but does it in a leaner format, adapted to slower mobile transmission speeds and scaled to a smaller screen. Finally, as this book goes to press, Digg is announcing yet another new feature, namely "a new advertising platform—Digg Ads." As Digg explains, "The more an ad is Dugg, the

digg

Recent 24hr 7days 30 365

Olive Garden **Never Ending** $8.95
Pasta Bowl
For a limited time. Dine in only. Pricing may vary in Canada.
Opinions? Click & Chance 2 win $250

91	Danish Woman Looking For Child's Father Is HOAX
79	Unwanted fat can be used as 'natural' breast implants
157	Money manager Jim Cramer vs. financial advisor Suze Orman
132	Meet the voice of Super Mario
218	Dawkins and Sagan: Will the Universe Be the New Religion?
134	Cracks in citizenship process result in man's deportation
91	Space robot 2.0: Smarter than the average rover
137	Britain tests water with microwave fish fingers
88	NBA Rookie of the Year Rankings: Preseason Edition
109	Plea to ease curbs on 'miracle' heroin drug

Use Regular Digg

Figure 1.3 The m.digg.com home page.

less the advertiser will have to pay. Conversely the more an ad is buried, the more the advertiser is charged, pricing it out of the system."

Web2.0 applications like Digg.com are making available untold amounts of information to Internet users. And they do so in ways that allow users to identify and focus on relevant information without getting lost in a sea of digital data. With so much information and with such rapidly changing technological means to navigate this information, it stands to reason that individuals without Internet access and without Internet competencies will get left out in the cold. When scholars and policy makers first began speaking of a "digital divide," the information and tools on the Internet were rather limited. One could take or leave Internet technology without being culturally, politically, or economically marginalized. This may be less true today as Web2.0 engages Internet users in more intense and interactive ways. What are the consequences for those who can't keep up with the rapid pace of Internet technology? And what are the consequences for those who aren't even on the Internet to begin with?

Inequality on the Web

In its early days, the Internet reflected the values of a relatively small group of users, primarily scientists, who emphasized collaboration and open access. As the Internet has evolved and gained in popularity, however, it has taken on the values of the larger society, which emphasize competition, status, and hierarchy. In this way, it has reproduced rather than challenged existing forms of inequality. Specifically, it has produced a new and quite powerful means by which social groups either gain or lose competitive advantage, in much the same way that schools facilitate our system of social stratification. One of the primary forms of inequality that we see is a lack of basic Internet access. Without some form of Internet access, the information and communication "revolution" that many associate with the Internet is meaningless. This lack of access is dangerous to the extent that it creates a new means of social exclusion.

With the majority of the U.S. adult population now enjoying some form of Internet access, however, this type of exclusion is becoming less problematic. We argue, therefore, that researchers and policy makers should be equally if not more concerned with inequalities that manifest among the population of Internet users. Among U.S. adults who enjoy some Internet access, there are significant differences in who enjoys consistent and continuous Internet access, in who possesses various Internet competencies, and in who finds relevant information on the Internet. As a result, individuals may have more or less access to valuable information, more or less ability to manage that information, and more or less use for that information.

The sheer volume of information available through the Internet has been a major issue at least since the mid-1990s. At that time, standards to facilitate the search and retrieval of Web documents were raised (RFC#1630) and the Uniform Resource Locator (URL) was introduced to standardize the web address system. RFC#1290, some 20 pages long, catalogued online libraries, bulletin boards, and directories, articulating the fundamental information issue:

> Attempting to make this wealth of information available to those who would find it useful poses some problems. First, we need to know of its existence . . . Second, even if you know of a document's existence, you may not know if it is important or relevant . . . Finally, once the existence and importance are known, the information needs to be indexed so that researchers can find it.

In short, the unanticipated growth in Internet content had the unforeseen consequence of information overload. Questions of navigation techniques, content relevancy, and organizational structure came to the fore as a result.

Web2.0 was designed to accommodate these issues. The collective intelligence of an ever expanding user base, for example, provides a means to organize and master the volume and magnitude of data. "Tagging," or the categorizing of Internet content using keywords, is another way that Internet users manage online data. Indeed, the value of many Web2.0 applications comes from the way in which they are able to focus a user's attention on relevant information, where relevance is defined by a user's stated interests and preferences, a user's past preferences and behavior, and the interests, preferences, and behavior of like-minded individuals. But in seeking to resolve the information processing dilemma, Web2.0 created new problems. Although Web2.0 has become a repository of collective intelligence, a platform for information-sharing, and a vehicle for collective interaction and expression, it has the potential to alienate anyone without consistent Internet access, anyone without a certain level of Internet savvy, and anyone without an interest in the kinds of information brought to the Internet.

Examples from the Internet may help illustrate this point. Google "replace Volvo XC70 headlight" and you get http://helpfulvideo.com/

video/show/760/how-to-remove-headlight-in-volvo-s70-v70-xc70.html, a very helpful step-by-step, how-to-do video demonstration. But this information is only relevant if your Internet connection is consistent and your Internet speed is sufficient to watch a video. Interested in finding an assessment of your child's school, you may stumble upon www.greatschools.net, which hosts parents' discussions on school-related issues and parents' reviews of schools. But if your child attends a school in which the majority of students lack Internet access at home, you're unlikely to find parents of students at that school actively discussing the strengths and weaknesses of the school online. In need of medical information, you can go to the webMD site (www.webmd.com), a repository of articles on medical topics and discussion boards frequented by patients and caregivers. But featured topics that get the most traffic are likely to be those that resonate with the middle-class users who frequent the Internet, not topics like "lead poisoning," which would be of greater concern to low-income users.

In the end, Web2.0 works best for the Internet everyman or everywoman, who tends to be educated and well-off. Thus, in addition to restricting information to those who have access to the Internet, Web2.0 restricts relevant information to those who are most similar to that typical Internet user. As you read about some of the major sociological perspectives of the Internet and consider empirical data on Internet use, think carefully about what kind of information is available on the web, how users actually access that information, and what skills they need to access and sift through that information. In doing so, you'll be better able to understand inequalities in information access, information processing, and information relevance.

Organization of the Book

In the next chapter, we'll take a closer look at differences in Internet use among the U.S. adult population. Specifically, we'll consider how online activity varies with gender, age, race, education, employment, and income. In the chapters that follow, we'll apply three different sociological perspectives to explore the relevance of these differences. All of these perspectives agree on this point: technology adoption and adaptation occur in particular socio-historical circumstances, which give shape to the organization and structure of that technology.

Apart from this common understanding, the three perspectives have different explanations for social inequality:

- The conflict perspective, originating with the work of Karl Marx, pinpoints the root of inequality in class relations under capitalism. This perspective holds that ownership of valuable resources, including skill assets, puts certain social classes at a distinct advantage. Thus, individuals with significant Internet competencies might enjoy a privileged position under capitalism. Institutions like the family and educational system reproduce those privileges over time, such that individuals in higher social classes will learn Internet skills and competencies that will give them a competitive advantage.
- The cultural perspective, derived from the work of Max Weber, emphasizes multiple sources of inequality in modern society: notably, class and status. These sources of inequality manifest not simply in terms of differences in economic resources and political power, but in terms of lifestyle and life conduct. Thus, individuals with more prestige and higher social status will enjoy greater access to the Internet and will consolidate their esteemed status through social networking on the Internet. Internet-based interaction constitutes a type of lifestyle that defines high status groups and works to their advantage.
- The functionalist perspective, with its origins in Emile Durkheim's work, accepts social inequality as a legitimate price to pay for the contributions that prestigious individuals make to society. Specifically, complex societies have a division of labor, in which individuals specialize in different tasks according to their abilities and interests. As an incentive for some individuals to specialize in tasks that are functionally important in society, the social structure provides material and social rewards. Thus, savvy Internet users will find Internet information more relevant and more useful in securing some social or economic return. But this

inequality will be justified to the extent that these users provide valuable social goods in the form of ideas, products, and services.

Each of these sociological perspectives offers its own insights into the relationship between the Internet and inequality. Thus, for each, we'll present relevant theoretical material, coupled with empirical data to test the explanatory potential of each perspective. In the concluding chapter, we'll tie the three perspectives together indicating how collectively they provide us with a better understanding of the digital divide than any one perspective alone. In this final chapter, we'll also turn to questions of public policy and how policy might be informed by these sociological analyses of the Internet.

Questions for Reading, Reflection, and Debate

1 Make a list of everything you have done on the Internet in the last week. How would you have accomplished those tasks without the Internet? What did these tasks provide you in economic, political, and social terms? Had you not accomplished these tasks, what effect would it have on your life in the short and long term?

2 Visit the RFC website at www.rfc-editor.org and look up three RFCs: #3751, #1097, and #1438. What is each of these RFCs about? Looking at the dates on which each RFC was published, can you find a common link? (Here's a hint: it's not a national holiday, but it is a nationally significant day.) What does this information tell us about the architects of the Internet? What kind of group is this and how might their flippant style have affected the Internet's development?

3 Pick one of the following Internet sites to peruse and analyze: www.JamBase.com, www.flickr.com, or www.Instructables.com. Using Figure 1.1, which illustrates differences in Web1.0 and Web2.0, discuss how the site conforms (or does not conform) to the major features of Web2.0. What characteristics might members of these sites have in common? And what kind of return might they enjoy from their use of these sites?

2
INTERNET USE AMONG
AMERICAN ADULTS

The Internet is becoming an increasingly vital tool in our information society. More Americans are going online to conduct such day-to-day activities as education, business transactions, personal correspondence, research and information-gathering, and job searches. Each year, being digitally connected becomes ever more critical to economic and educational advancement and community participation. Now that a large number of Americans regularly use the Internet to conduct daily activities, people who lack access to these tools are at a growing disadvantage. Therefore, raising the level of digital inclusion by increasing the number of Americans using the technology tools of the digital age is a vitally important national goal.

—*NTIA* 2000

Introduction

The picture in the May 30, 2009 online edition of the *Wall Street Journal* was a curious one. In it, a black man wearing baggy, worn pants and an untrimmed beard is sitting in what looks to be a bus terminal, a sleek laptop perched on his lap. While he concentrates on the computer screen, a man sleeps next to him on the wooden bench. We do not see the sleeping man's face; it is buried underneath a dirty coat and sandwiched between two trash bags. It turns out that the terminal is San Francisco's Transbay Terminal and the men are two members of the city's homeless community. Although he is homeless, the man featured

ﬞ the laptop has accounts on Facebook, MySpace, and Twitter. He ɔ runs an Internet forum on Yahoo! and communicates regularly ith family and friends by email. Even on the streets, the accompanyng article proclaims, "the homeless stay wired" (Dvorak 2009).

Could it be that everyone, even San Francisco's homeless population, is online? Is Internet access and use really that ubiquitous? Or are there differences in who has access to the Internet, who uses it regularly, and who uses it for particular activities? These are empirical questions that can not be answered by interviewing a handful of homeless men who happen to be privy to a laptop and some electricity. Rather than relying on exceptional cases to uncover social trends, social scientists analyze large data sets, which are much more representative of social phenomena than are non-randomly selected cases. In this chapter, I will use data from the Pew Internet & American Life Project to examine U.S. Internet use from 2000 to 2007. This project, an initiative of the Pew Research Center, has collected telephone survey data on American Internet use since March of 2000. Survey participants are randomly selected from a list of phone numbers for all U.S. households with a telephone. Beginning in December 2008, cell phone numbers were included in this list. The project makes its data and a variety of reports based on the data publicly available at www.pewinternet.org.

Using this data, we'll analyze who is using the Internet, how often they're using it, and what they're doing online. According to Pew survey data, the percentage of American adults who had ever been on the Internet increased from 46 percent to 71 percent between 2000 and 2007. In addition, those Americans who had used the Internet on the day prior to being interviewed increased from just under one in three adults to just under one in two adults. Although these figures indicate growing Internet use, such growth tends to be concentrated among certain groups. As well, there are differences in what American adults do online. Thus, in the first half of this chapter, we'll describe differences in Internet use by gender, age, race, ethnicity, education, employment status, and income. In the second half of this chapter, we'll take a close look at what people do online and how this varies by the demographic characteristics discussed in the first half of the chapter.

Demographics of Internet Use

Tables 2.1 and 2.2 provide a basic demographic description of the Pew samples in 2000 and 2007. These numbers suggest that these samples are fairly representative of the overall U.S. population. It's important to note, however, that there tend to be gender, race, and educational differences between individuals who agree to participate in surveys and individuals who refuse to participate. This makes these samples less representative of the overall U.S. population than they would otherwise be using random sampling methods. To account for this possible selection bias, we use weighted estimates. Using these techniques, we can be confident that these are representative estimates for the U.S. adult population, with a margin of error in most cases of about ±3 percent.

Table 2.1 Gender, Age, and Race of Pew Internet & American Life Samples, 2000 and 2007

	2000 PEW SAMPLE (%)[1]	2007 PEW SAMPLE (%)[2]
Gender		
Male	47.7	47.8
Female	52.3	52.2
Age		
18–24 years old	12.9	11.1
25–34 years old	19.0	16.5
35–44 years old	22.5	19.5
45–54 years old	17.9	19.8
55–64 years old	11.3	14.5
65 years or older	15.9	16.8
don't know/refused	2.1	1.7
Race		
white	82.3	76.0
black	10.9	12.4
Asian	1.1	3.3
other/mixed	3.2	5.0
don't know/refused	2.4	3.2

Percentages may not equal 100% due to rounding.

Notes:

1 Sample size is 3,533. The reported margin of error is ±2.5% for demographic items from this survey and ±3% for items on specific Internet activities (Pew Internet & American Life Project 2000).

2 Sample size is 2,200. The reported margin of error is ±2.3% for demographic items from this survey and ±2.8% for items on specific Internet activities (Rainie and Tancer 2007).

2.2 Educational Level, Employment Status, and Family Income of Pew Internet & American Life Samples, 2000 and 2007

	2000 PEW SAMPLE (%)[1]	2007 PEW SAMPLE (%)[2]
Educational Level		
Less than high school degree	15.4	13.7
High school graduate	36.9	31.8
Some college	23.4	26.5
Bachelor's degree or higher	23.7	27.0
Don't know/refused	0.9	1.0
Employment Status		
Employed full-time	55.3	49.4
Employed part-time	10.5	11.6
Retired	18.4	20.6
Not employed for pay	11.8	13.7
Other	3.2	4.1
Don't know/refused	0.8	0.7
Family Income		
Less than $10,000	6.2	7.4
$10,000 to under $20,000	10.1	8.0
$20,000 to under $30,000	12.2	9.7
$30,000 to under $40,000	11.7	8.1
$40,000 to under $50,000	9.4	7.9
$50,000 to under $75,000	14.0	13.2
$75,000 to under $100,000	7.0	10.4
$100,000 or more	6.6	11.0
Don't know/refused	22.9	24.3

Percentages may not equal 100% due to rounding.

Notes:

1 Sample size is 3,533. The reported margin of error is ±2.5% for demographic items from this survey and ±3% for items on specific Internet activities (Pew Internet & American Life Project 2000).

2 Sample size is 2,200. The reported margin of error is ±2.3% for demographic items from this survey and ±2.8% for items on specific Internet activities (Rainie and Tancer 2007).

This section considers how Internet use varies among individuals in this sample according to various demographic and socio-economic characteristics. Specifically, we'll look closely at gender, age, race, education, employment, and income to see whether differences in Internet use emerge along these social dimensions.

Figure 2.1 maps the overall increase in American adults who have ever been online (the upper solid line) and the overall increase in adults who

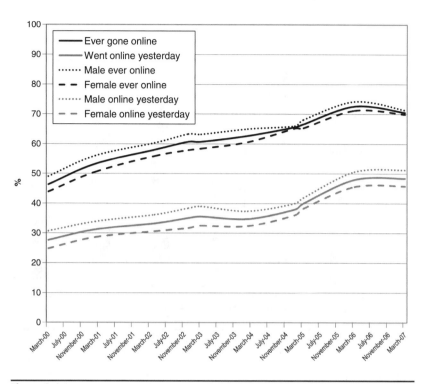

Figure 2.1 Internet use among American adults by gender, 2000–2007.

went online the day before being surveyed (the lower solid line). Although over 70 percent of American adults had used the Internet in 2007, just under half had used it the day prior to being interviewed by the Pew Internet & American Life Project. Thus, although the Internet has undoubtedly become an important part of contemporary American life, it is not yet an important part of *daily* life for roughly half of all American adults. Layered alongside these overall trends, the dashed and dotted lines in Figure 2.1 trace the male and female trends in Internet use, respectively. As these lines indicate, male and female levels of Internet use have converged in recent years. In 2000, for example, the difference in male–female Internet use was statistically significant; by 2007, that difference was statistically indistinguishable. We can say, then, that U.S. adult men and women are using the Internet at more or less equal rates, such that gender is not a major digital divide in terms of Internet use.

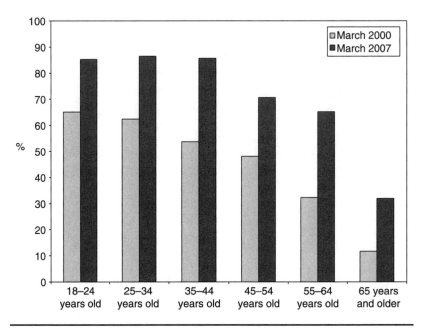

Figure 2.2 American adults who ever used the Internet by age, 2000 and 2007.

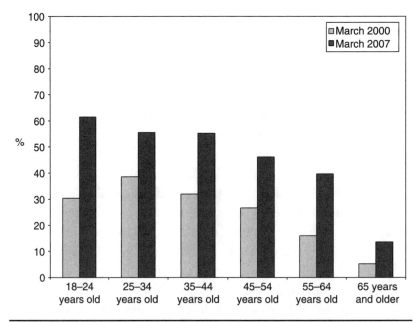

Figure 2.3 American adults who used the Internet on previous day by age, 2000 and 2007.

Figures 2.2 and 2.3 present age-related trends in Internet use among American adults. Here, too, we note increasing percentages of use across all age categories, both among those who had ever used the Internet and among those who had used the Internet the previous day. Among the three youngest age groups (18–24 years, 25–34 years, and 35–44 years), over half had been online in 2000 and over 85 percent had been online as of 2007. By 2007, we see very little difference in Internet use among these age groups. In contrast, significantly lower percentages of individuals in the older age groups (45–54 years and 55–64 years) reported any online experience, though the gap between the younger and older age groups closed considerably between 2000 and 2007. About one-third of those aged 55 to 64 reported any online experience in 2000, compared to about two-thirds of those aged 18 to 24. By 2007, this disparity had been cut significantly, with about 65 percent of those aged 55 to 64 reporting online experience, compared to about 85 percent of Americans aged 18 to 24. The most striking age-based disparity in Internet use lies with those age 65 and older. In 2000, just over 10 percent of Americans in this age group had been ever been online. By 2007, that number had increased to approximately 30 percent. Even so, older Americans' online participation rates lagged well behind the next youngest cohort and further still behind all other adult Americans in 2007.[1]

Looking at Figure 2.4, we see that the percentage of American adults who had ever used the Internet also varied by race in 2000 and 2007. Comparing black and white adult Internet use in 2000, we find a 13 percent difference between the two groups. In 2007, the reported percentage of black Americans who had ever been online increased to 60 percent, compared to 73 percent of white Americans. Thus, although online experience increased for both blacks and whites, the increase was relatively similar, leaving the gap between blacks and whites unchanged. Figure 2.5 shows a very similar pattern for Internet use on the day prior to interview. An increase in the percentage of adults who used the Internet on the previous day is found for both black and white adults between 2000 and 2007. The percentage of blacks increased from 13 to 33 percent; the percentage of whites

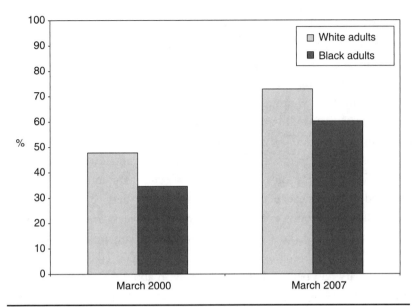

Figure 2.4 American adults who ever used the Internet by race, 2000 and 2007.

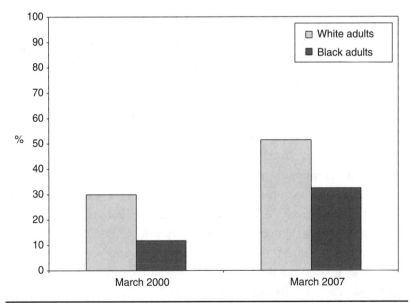

Figure 2.5 American adults who used the Internet on previous day by race, 2000 and 2007.

increased from 30 to just over 50 percent. Since the share of both groups increased by 20 percent, however, the racial gap in Internet use on the previous day remained unchanged during this time period.

As Figures 2.6 and 2.7 indicate, Internet use continues to be correlated with level of education. The proportion of American adults without a high school degree who had ever used the Internet more than doubled between 2000 and 2007. Nevertheless, only 40 percent of those without a high school degree had ever been online in 2007, compared with over 90 percent of those with at least a bachelor's degree. That same year, less than one-quarter of those without a high school degree had used the Internet on the day prior to being surveyed, compared with approximately three-quarters of those with at least a bachelor's degree. The educational disparity in ever using the Internet was greater in 2000 than in 2007, but the gap had narrowed only moderately by 2007. More importantly, the education gap in those who used the Internet on the previous day actually *increased* between 2000 and 2007, suggesting a growing educational divide in consistent or daily Internet use. These results indicate that America's colleges provide important educational and social experiences that promote Internet use.

Figures 2.8 and 2.9 suggest that full-time employment is also associated with Internet use.[2] Between 2000 and 2007, the percentage of employed adults who had ever been online increased from 56 to 82 percent. Among those who were neither employed nor retired, whose Internet use was consistently lower, Internet experience also increased from 43 to 70 percent. The gap in Internet experience between the employed and the neither employed nor retired, however, remained virtually unchanged between 2000 and 2007. Online participation among retired adults increased from 18 percent in 2000 to 42 percent in 2007. In this case, however, the disparity between employed and retired persons who had ever been online actually *increased* from 38 to 40 percent. Looking at those individuals who reported that they had used the Internet on the previous day, we see similar results. In 2007, 60 percent of American adults who were employed full-time used the Internet on the previous day, compared with 44 percent of those who were neither employed nor retired and 24 percent of those who were

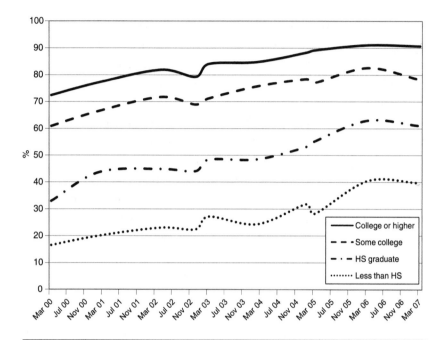

Figure 2.6 American adults who ever used the Internet by education, 2000–2007.

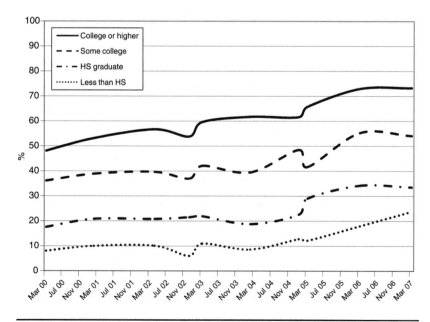

Figure 2.7 American adults who used the Internet on previous day by education, 2000–2007.

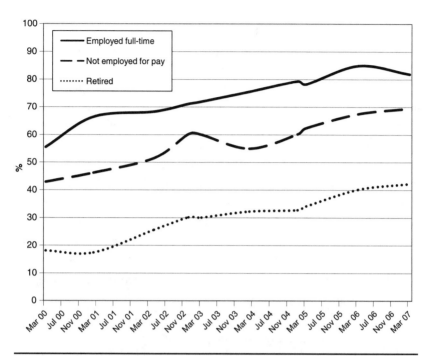

Figure 2.8 American adults who ever used the Internet by employment status, 2000–2007.

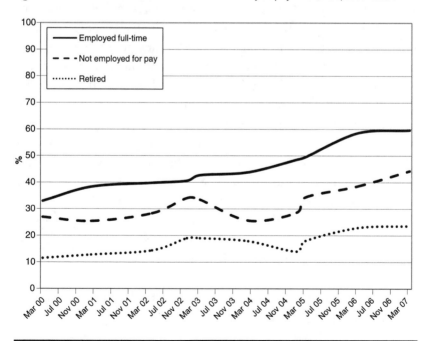

Figure 2.9 American adults who used the Internet on previous day by employment status, 2000–2007.

retired. Reported Internet use on the previous day grew most rapidly for those who were employed, suggesting that employment status is becoming a major factor in determining Internet use.

The role that employment plays in Internet use can be seen by looking in more detail at individual responses regarding use of the Internet on the previous day. In April of 2000, 791 of the 2,503 individuals interviewed by the Pew Project were surveyed on a Sunday or a Monday, that is, on days when they were unlikely to have been at work the previous day. In March of 2007, 620 of the 2,200 individuals interviewed were surveyed on a Sunday or Monday. Considering that Internet use might be higher for employed adults on days when they are at work, interviewing adults on a Sunday or Monday might skew the results and the effect of employment status since the previous day would have been a Saturday or Sunday (i.e., non-work days). Here, we want to separate those adults interviewed on a Sunday or Monday from those adults interviewed on other days so that we can get a better sense of differences in Internet use on the previous day.

Table 2.3 summarizes Internet use in 2000 and in 2007 by employment status and day of the week. In both years, regardless of employment status, we find that reported Internet use was more common during the week than on weekends. At both time points, however, this difference is only statistically significant for employed individuals. These differences are slightly less pronounced in 2007 than in 2000. Regardless of the day of the week, Internet use the previous day remains far more common among the employed than those not employed in both years. Thus, it is not simply greater access to the Internet that the employed enjoy at work; if it were, we would find differences in Internet use during the week and not during the weekend among the employed. Instead, we find that the employed are far more likely to be online the day prior to being interviewed regardless of whether that previous day was during the week or weekend. The employed, therefore, are more likely to use the Internet consistently for other reasons.

As Figures 2.10 and 2.11 show, the relationship between income and Internet use is significant. Consistently between 2000 and 2007,

Table 2.3 Internet Use on Previous Day by Employment Status and Day of the Week, 2000 and 2007

DID YOU GO ONLINE YESTERDAY. . .

	EMPLOYED, YESTERDAY WAS. . .[1]		NOT EMPLOYED, YESTERDAY WAS. . .[2]	
2000	weekday	weekend	weekday	weekend
Yes	37.0%	26.3%	17.5%	17.2%
No	63.0%	73.7%	82.5%	82.8%
	100.0%	100.0%	100.0%	100.0%
	EMPLOYED, YESTERDAY WAS. . .[3]		NOT EMPLOYED, YESTERDAY WAS. . .[4]	
2007	weekday	weekend	weekday	weekend
Yes	61.9%	51.6%	32.6%	29.4%
No	38.1%	48.4%	67.4%	70.6%
	100.0%	100.0%	100.0%	100.0%

Source: April 2000 Tracking Survey, March 2007 Tracking Survey.
Notes:
1 Number of surveys = 1,686, χ^2 = 21.00, p < 0.01.
2 Number of surveys = 797, χ^2 =0.08 p = 0.78.
3 Number of surveys = 1,214, χ^2 = 11.18, p > 0.01.
4 Number of surveys = 970, χ^2 =1.83, p= 0.176.

reported levels of Internet use increase in proportion to reported household income. And in each successively higher income group, we find higher reported levels of Internet use. Looking a bit more closely, however, the relationship between Internet use and income becomes more complex. In Figure 2.10, we see that between 2000 and 2007, the gap between the percentage of the poorest Americans and the wealthiest Americans who had ever been online remained large, but had narrowed. In 2000, 81 percent of those in households with incomes of $100,000 or more had ever been online, compared to 26 percent of those in households with incomes under $10,000. In 2007, 93 percent of those in the wealthiest households had ever been online, compared with 45 percent of those in the poorest households. The difference in percentage points went from 55 in 2000 to 48 in 2007, indicating a slightly narrower but still significant income divide.

Figure 2.11, which traces the relationship between income and use of the Internet on the day prior to interview, shows an *increasing* gap between the poorest and the wealthiest Americans between 2000 and 2007. The percentage of respondents in the poorest households who

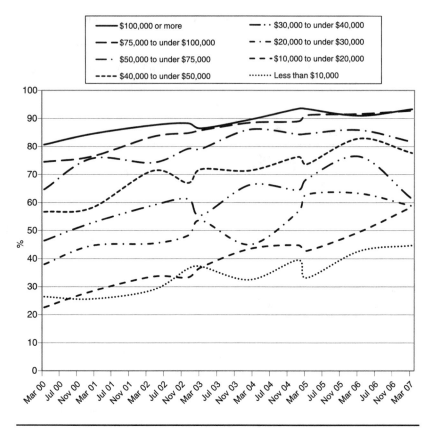

Figure 2.10 American adults who ever used the Internet by income, 2000–2007.

reported Internet use on the prior day increased from 15 to 25 percent during this time frame. The percentage of respondents from the wealthiest households, however, increased at a faster rate, from 53 percent in 2000 to 77 percent in 2007. In this case, then, the difference in percentage points increased from 38 in 2000 to 52 in 2007, indicating a growing divide between the wealthiest and poorest in terms of consistent Internet use.

As we consider these demographic characteristics, it is important to remember that these characteristics can not be understood in isolation. There are no "men" or "women" in the real world, but rather men or women of a particular age, race, class, and so on. Looking at particular

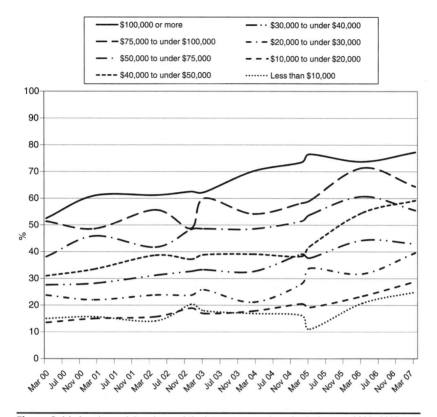

Figure 2.11 American adults who used the Internet on previous day by income, 2000–2007.

combinations of these characteristics allows us to capture differences in Internet use in a manner that is closer to how we experience them in the real world. We might compare, for example, black adults age 65 or older with a high school degree or less to white adults age 25 to 34 with a bachelor's degree or higher to examine the intersection of these variables and their relation to digital inequality. Were we to make such a comparison, we would find that only 2 percent of the first group had ever used the Internet in 2000, compared with 85 percent of the second group. By 2006, an estimated 13 percent of blacks in the first group had used the Internet, compared with 96 percent of whites in the comparison group (Fox and Livingston 2007). For both groups, Internet use has become more prevalent. But a gap in Internet use between the two groups remains.

Further examples of the combined impact of demographic variables may be seen in Figure 2.12. This figure suggests that education trumps race and ethnicity to some extent in conferring digital advantage and disadvantage. Roughly 90 percent of all college graduates used the Internet in 2006, regardless of race or ethnicity. In fact, a greater percentage of black college graduates (93 percent) used the Internet in 2006 than white college graduates (91 percent). (Hispanic college graduates had the lowest percentage of Internet use at 89 percent.) At the other extreme, only about 30 percent of those without a high school

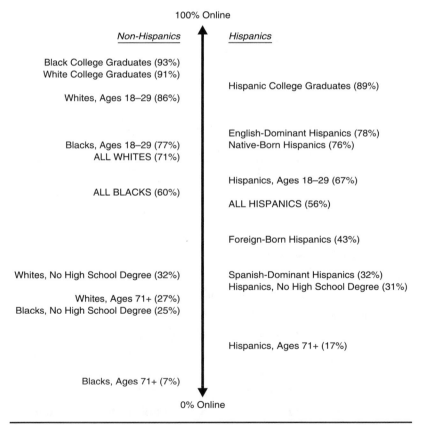

Figure 2.12 Internet use by demographic group, 2006 (source: Fox and Livingston 2007).

degree use the Internet, again regardless of race or ethnicity. To some extent, age also trumps race and ethnicity, with less than 30 percent of adults aged 71 years and older using the Internet in 2006, regardless of race and ethnicity. Here, the effects of race are stronger, with 27 percent of whites aged 71 and older using the Internet in 2006, compared with 17 and 7 percent of Hispanics and blacks in this age group, respectively. Conversely, over two-thirds of all racial-ethnic groups age 18 to 29 used the Internet in 2006. A greater percentage of whites in this age group used the Internet (86 percent) compared with blacks (77 percent) and Hispanics (67 percent). Figure 2.12 also shows that, among Hispanics, Internet use was more prevalent in 2006 among those whose primary language was English and those who were born in the United States. In this sense, Internet use appears to be tied to assimilation.

Demographics of Online Activities

Tracking Internet use across different demographic groups indicates important differences in who uses the Internet and how often. But there may also be 'digital divides' in online activities. Among American Internet users, who does what online? The Pew Internet & American Life Project collects ongoing data about the online activities of American Internet users. Table 2.4 lists the ten most common activities reported by Internet users in surveys conducted between 2000 and 2005.[3] Topping the list in 2000 and 2005 is sending or receiving email (91 percent of all Internet users). Looking at the remainder of the list, email stands out as the only online activity related to communication. With the exception of going online "for no particular reason, just for fun or to pass the time" and going online to purchase a product, all other items on the list in Table 2.4 relate to obtaining information. Indeed, in 2005, "searching for information" was as common an activity as sending or receiving email (again, 91 percent of all Internet users).

In 2000 and 2005, two consumer-oriented activities appear among the top ten online activities. In 2000, 74 percent of Internet users reported doing online research on products and services and 64 percent reporting using the Internet to get information about ticket and hotel prices. Both consumer activities increased through 2005. By 2005,

Table 2.4 Most Common Online Activities, 2000–2005

1	Send or read email	91%	3/2000	Send or read email	91%	3/2005
2	Do an internet search to find the answer to a specific question	79%	10/2000	Use an online search engine to help find information on the Web	91%	12/2005
3	Search for a map or driving directions	78%	8/2001	Search for a map or driving directions	84%	2/2004
4	Look for information about a hobby or interest	76%	3/2000	Research a product or service online	78%	3/2005
5	Research a product or service online	74%	3/2000	Check weather reports and forecasts	78%	11/2004
6	Get information about travel (e.g., airline ticket prices or hotel rates)	64%	3/2000	Look for information about a hobby or interest	77%	11/2004
7	Go online for no particular reason, just for fun or to pass the time	63%	3/2000	Get information about travel (e.g., airline ticket prices or hotel rates)	73%	6/2004
8	Check weather reports and forecasts	62%	3/2000	Get news online	68%	3/2005
9	Look for information about movies, music, books, or other leisure activities	62%	3/2000	Buy a product online	67%	6/2005
10	Get news online	60%	3/2000	Go online for no particular reason, just for fun or to pass the time	66%	12/2005

Source: Pew Internet & American Life Tracking Surveys.

online purchasing also appears on the top ten Internet activities. During that year, two-thirds of the Pew survey respondents reported that they had used the Internet to purchase products such as books, music, toys, or clothing. Rounding out the list of most common online activities in 2005, we also see that over two-thirds of Internet users used the Internet as a source of news. Because of the way that news is typically presented to online readers, with advertisements for products and services, we can assume that this particular activity also has a consumer component.

Table 2.5 lists those online activities with rapid rates of growth in recent years.[4] These data suggest that Internet users are increasingly

Table 2.5 Online Activities with Recent Growth, 2000–2006

	PERCENT OF USERS AT FIRST TIME MEASURED		PERCENT OF USERS AT TIME LAST MEASURED		YEARLY RATE OF INCREASE
Read someone else's web log or blog	17%	2/2004	39%	1/2006	11.5%
Use a wireless device to go online	17%	2/2004	25%	11/2004	10.7%
Use online social or professional networking sites like LinkedIn	7%	3/2005	11%	9/2005	8.0%
Get information or support from sites for medical condition or personal situations	47%	9/2002	58%	11/2004	5.1%
Look for news or information about politics and the campaign	35%	3/2000	58%	11/2004	4.9%
Buy or make a reservation for travel	36%	3/2000	63%	9/2005	4.9%
Bank online	17%	3/2000	43%	12/2005	4.5%
Buy a product online	48%	3/2000	67%	6/2005	3.6%
Check weather reports and forecasts	62%	3/2000	78%	11/2004	3.4%
Get photos developed/store or display photos	20%	8/2001	34%	9/2005	3.4%
Rate a product, service or person using an online rating system	26%	6/2004	30%	9/2005	3.2%
Make a donation to a charity online	7%	11/2001	18%	9/2005	2.9%
Download video files onto your computer	13%	11/2003	18%	12/2005	2.4%
Search for a map or driving directions	78%	8/2001	84%	2/2004	2.4%
Get information about travel	64%	3/2000	73%	6/2004	2.1%
Take a class online just for personal enjoyment or enrichment	5%	2/2001	13%	1/2005	2.0%

Source: Pew Internet & American Life Surveys, 2000 through 2006.

taking advantage of the Internet's communications capabilities beyond email. The proportion of Pew respondents who said they read blogs more than doubled between 2004 and 2006. Blogs are geared toward communicating with family, friends, and acquaintances in an open-diary format. Some blogs reach a larger readership and may be more news-oriented, although the style typically remains informal and familiar. Social networking sites are also growing in popularity, with 11 percent of all Internet users reporting in September of 2005 that they had visited such sites, an 8 percent increase from just six months prior.

Many of the types of growing Internet use revolve around web sites that are explicitly commercial. As noted above, online purchasing is now among the most commonly reported uses of the Internet. In 2004, 67 percent of adult American Internet users used the Internet to purchase a product or service, up from under 50 percent in 2000. Similar rates of increased use are found in online banking, travel purchases and reservations, and photo services. A relatively rapid increase in the use of product ratings was also reported during this time. And nearly all of the other activities listed in Table 2.5 contain some form of advertising. Thus, even when users are not seeking product information or making an actual purchase, advertising infuses non-commercial sites with a commercial component. For example, Internet users who search for driving directions at Mapquest.com will find travel-related advertising and offers.

In another example of the ubiquity of advertising on the web, the leading source for video downloading, YouTube, not only places advertising on its pages, but features advertisements in its video offerings. Indeed, some of the most obvious examples of advertising are found in the "Community" section of YouTube, where many of the "Groups" are fans and promoters of particular entertainers. Further, and as Figure 2.13 illustrates, many of the featured "Contests" are thinly veiled advertisements. The "Moms Can Do Anything" video contest, for example, is organized by WalMart. The "Save Money, Save Energy, Win Big" video contest, which depicts a smiling woman in an orange apron, is sponsored by Home Depot. The "Kraft Cooking Video Challenge" asks viewers to submit videos of themselves preparing

Figure 2.13 Sample of YouTube community page, 2008.

particular dishes that use Kraft ingredients. These online contests, innocuous on the surface, allow WalMart, Home Depot, Kraft, and many other companies to advertise at little or no cost.

In the list of rapidly increasing uses of the Internet, advertising is least prominent on charitable organization websites. Online charitable donating has experienced a 3 percent rate of growth between 2001 and 2005. Yet even on charitable sites, advertising is often just a click away. For example, in the summer of 2007, the Kidney Foundation's website included a prominent story of an upcoming charity golf event at the Pebble Beach Country Club. A user who clicked on the banner for the event was then sent to the golfing event page, which contained logos of the event's sponsors, including *Golf Digest*, the Pebble Beach Company, and Cingular wireless. Clicking on another upcoming event, the U.S. Transplant Games, led to a page that included information on event advertisers and exhibitors. Thus, even non-profit web sites are steeped in commercial content.

If we think about communication and information as the two primary dimensions of online activities, and juxtapose these with production and consumption as two primary dimensions of economic activity,[5] we come up with four combinations:

1 Online communication oriented toward production.
2 Online communication oriented toward consumption.
3 Online information-seeking oriented toward consumption.
4 Online information-seeking oriented toward production.

Figure 2.14 takes these four combinations and identifies specific online activities associated with each. Along the communication-information axis, email is at the communication end, but this communication may concern production or consumption. Online searching is at the information end of the axis, but may also be related to production or consumption. Using the Internet at work is on the production end of the axis, but this activity may be related to communication or information-seeking. Buying a product is at the consumption end of the axis, but buying a product may involve online information-seeking and online communication.

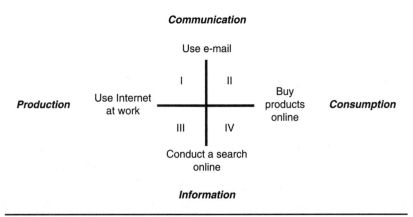

Figure 2.14 Dimensions of Internet activity.

Looking at Table 2.6, we see how these online activities varied by gender, age, race, education, and household income in 2005. Overall participation rates are greatest for email (over 90 percent) and least for using the Internet at work (just over 50 percent). Significant gender differences are found only in the activity most closely associated with production, namely using the Internet at work, with women less likely

Table 2.6 Demographic and Socio-economic Differences in Internet Activities, 2005

PERCENTAGE OF INTERNET USERS WHO . . .	SEND OR READ EMAIL (%)	ONLINE SEARCH (%)	BUY PRODUCTS ONLINE (%)	WORK OTHER THAN EMAIL (%)
Total	91.2	90.5	67.0	50.3
Gender				
Male	90.5	91.1	67.6	53.8*
Female	91.9	90.0	66.4	46.9
Age				
18–24 years old	86.9	88.8*	65.5*	37.3
25–34 years old	92.8	93.8	71.9	55.4
35–44 years old	94.4	92.2	68.5	57.3
45–54 years old	90.0	92.0	66.5	58.8
55–64 years old	90.5	88.0	68.3	46.1
65 years or older	93.0	82.0	48.1	21.9
Race				
White	92.4*	91.5	69.0*	51.3*
Black	83.8	84.1	55.8	39.8
Asian	100.0	100.0	59.1	65.2
Other/mixed	86.2	85.8	63.6	42.3
Educational Achievement				
Less than high school degree	78.9*	74.9*	36.7*	23.9*
High school graduate	85.7	84.8	59.1	34.3
Some college	93.2	91.9	67.8	47.4
Bachelor's degree or higher	96.3	96.3	78.0	70.6
Household Income				
Less than $20,000	80.9*	86.2*	59.2*	32.6*
$20,000 to under $30,000	84.9	89.5	48.8	36.6
$30,000 to under $40,000	90.3	89.6	63.2	42.2
$40,000 to under $75,000	95.2	90.5	69.7	52.1
$75,000 or more	94.9	95.6	80.0	67.7
Sample size	1,927	1,931	1,335	1,923

Source: Pew Internet & American Life Project survey December 2005.
Note:
* $p < 0.001$.

than men to use the Internet for this purpose.[6] The most significant age-related differences are primarily found for online searches and buying products online, with those over 65 years of age least likely to do each compared with other age groups. With the exception of online searching, there are also significant differences in online activities according to race. Blacks are least likely to use the Internet in all four respects; whites are most likely to use the Internet to buy products online; and Asians are most likely to use the Internet at work and to email. Finally, better educated and more affluent Internet users are more likely to participate in all four online activities when compared with less educated and less affluent users. Along the production/consumption axis, but also across the communication/information axis, we see that online activity is tied most to education and income.

Table 2.7 considers participation in four secondary online activities: taking an online class for credit, sending instant messages, playing games online, and going online "just for fun." As before, these data were collected in 2005. That year, women were more likely than men to take a class online. Younger Internet users (18–34 years) were more likely to take part in each activity compared with older users. With respect to race, Asians and blacks were more likely to send instant messages and play games than whites and other races. The more educated were more likely than the less educated to take a class online. Interestingly, the inverse is true for playing games online: as education increases, participation in online gaming declines. A similar relationship may be found between income and online gaming, with online gaming declining as income increases.

As we consider these variations in Internet activities, we need to keep in mind the differences in Internet use that we found in the first half of this chapter. If you don't have access to the Internet or otherwise don't use the Internet, you don't email, you don't search online for information, and you certainly don't take online classes for credit. The data presented in Tables 2.6 and 2.7 are based on responses to questions asked *only of Internet users.* To get a more accurate assessment of the degree of Internet inequality in America today, we need to bring those individuals who don't use the Internet back into the equation

Table 2.7 Demographic and Socio-economic Differences in Other Internet Activities, 2005

PERCENTAGE OF INTERNET USERS WHO ...	TAKE A CLASS ONLINE (%)	SEND INSTANT MESSAGES (%)	PLAY GAMES ONLINE (%)	GO ONLINE FOR FUN (%)
Total	11.5	36.9	30.9	66.4
Gender				
Male	10.0*	37.0	31.4	68.5
Female	13.0	36.8	30.4	64.4
Age				
18–24 years old	16.0*	59.8*	43.9*	80.6*
25–34 years old	16.9	41.3	35.8	79.2
35–44 years old	10.8	32.2	30.4	65.3
45–54 years old	10.2	31.1	24.2	59.9
55–64 years old	4.2	27.3	21.9	54.6
65 years or older	4.0	27.5	30.1	49.6
Race				
White	10.9	35.3*	29.1*	66.5
Black	16.9	49.0	47.6	65.4
Asian	13.5	64.0	34.8	78.7
Other/mixed	10.3	35.2	30.0	71.1
Educational Achievement				
Less than high school degree	3.6*	42.9	46.2*	66.4*
High school graduate	5.9	34.6	34.8	72.1
Some college	14.4	41.5	32.0	68.1
Bachelor's degree or higher	14.7	33.9	24.1	60.4
Household Income				
Less than $20,000	12.4	43.1	51.6*	71.6
$20,000 to under $30,000	12.3	37.0	47.5	67.3
$30,000 to under $40,000	8.9	42.5	33.4	74.0
$40,000 to under $75,000	13.1	33.7	28.4	65.2
$75,000 or more	12.1	39.0	25.3	67.5
Sample size	1,931	1,928	1,929	1,927

Source: Pew Internet & American Life Project survey December 2005.
Note:
* $p < 0.001$.

or, more precisely, back into the denominator. Instead of calculating percentages as:

% participating in online activity a

$$= \frac{\text{Number of members of group } j \text{ who do activity } a}{\text{Number of Internet users in group } j}$$

we will calculate percentages as follows:

% participating in online activity a

$$= \frac{\text{Number of members of group } j \text{ who do activity } a}{\text{Number of members in group } j}$$

In the second equation, we include Internet users and non-users to get a sense of the percentage of the overall population that participates in each Internet activity.

When we consider Internet non-users in the equation, we find even more startling results. For example, comparing participation rates across the highest levels and lowest levels of education in Table 2.8, we see that those with a bachelor's degree or higher were more than three times as likely to use email than those without a high school degree. They were more than five times as likely to use the Internet at work and nearly eight times more likely to bank online. Looking at the relationship between income and online activities in Table 2.9, we find that individuals in households with incomes above $75,000 a year were two times more likely to use email than individuals in households with incomes

Table 2.8 Participation* in Selected Internet Activities by Education, 2005

	ALL ADULTS (%)	SOME HIGH SCHOOL (%)	HIGH SCHOOL (%)	SOME COLLEGE (%)	BA OR HIGHER (%)
Email	64.9	28.3	53.1	75.1	87.2
Read blog	28.3	16.3	17.6	34.1	40.6
Download music/video	18.5	8.8	13.6	21.5	26.3
Buy product	45.8	10.6	36.0	52.3	69.6
Online banking	28.7	5.9	18.2	35.4	46.7
Product research	52.4	16.6	39.8	60.5	77.7
Online search	60.1	25.0	46.8	71.8	82.7
Product rating	16.4	5.4	9.7	21.2	25.9
Take class online	13.3	6.3	8.3	18.3	18.4
Use Internet at work	43.6	12.3	31.3	48.5	69.0
Share files	18.2	8.1	16.4	21.2	22.4
Write blog	9.8	11.3	5.5	12.4	11.6

Source: Pew Internet & American Life Project surveys, March/September, and December 2005.
Note: * $p < 0.05$.

Table 2.9 Participation* in Selected Internet Activities by Household Income, 2005

	LESS THAN $20,000 (%)	$20,000–$30,000 (%)	$30,000–$40,000 (%)	$40,000–$75,000 (%)	$75,000 OR MORE (%)
Email	36.7	51.1	66.6	76.1	87.7
Read blog	18.6	28.9	20.7	31.3	39.9
Download music/video	9.3	11.2	13.0	23.1	30.1
Buy product	23.3	30.3	47.1	56.9	74.4
Online banking	10.0	18.6	26.5	38.7	49.4
Product research	25.6	42.0	50.4	66.2	82.1
Online search	34.7	49.7	61.7	72.7	85.3
Product rating	9.5	9.9	15.5	20.5	29.5
Take class online	10.6	10.7	19.3	13.6	23.0
Use Internet at work	19.5	29.3	46.1	51.3	67.5
Share files	10.0	18.9	20.4	23.7	22.3
Write blog	5.8	13.4	9.0	9.1	13.4

Source: Pew Internet & American Life Project surveys, March/September, and December 2005.

Note: * $p < 0.05$.

under $20,000. They were more than three times as likely to use the Internet at work and nearly five times more likely to bank online.

Inequality and the Internet

In this chapter, we considered patterns in Internet use from 2000 to 2007. We analyzed such variables as gender, age, race, education, employment, and income, which have typically been associated with the "digital divide." In our analysis, we discovered that education and income explain much of the variation in Internet use, although age and race are also important factors. We also learned that as the Internet matures, a primary divide emerging is between those who use the Internet consistently and those who use the Internet intermittently, which we measured by assessing whether the respondent used the Internet the previous day. Simply asking individuals if they have ever gone online does not get at whether individuals are going online regularly, if not daily. This kind of inequality can not be captured by thinking of the issue in terms of "haves" and "have nots." In general, more affluent, college educated, younger, white Americans are more likely to go online regularly than the less well-off, less educated, older, non-white Americans. Although this gap has narrowed in some respects (e.g., age), it has stayed the same (e.g., race) and increased (e.g., education and income) in others.

In this chapter, we also moved beyond the issue of overall Internet use to examine *types* of Internet use, or variations in online activity. Using data from the Pew Internet & American Life Project, we identified ten online activities participated in by more than two-thirds of American Internet users. These activities included using the Internet to email, to search for driving directions, and to buy products. As we found, participation in many, if not most, of these activities is not uniformly distributed across the population of Internet users and not at all uniformly distributed across the population at large. The most consistent and striking sources of variation were, again, along the lines of education and income and, to a lesser but still significant extent, along the lines of age and race. Generally speaking, the less educated and less well-off were less likely to do most of the major online activities compared with the well-educated and well-off. The exception here were some of the secondary Internet activities, like going online for fun and to play games, in which the less educated and less well-off were more likely to participate.

How do we explain these differences in Internet use? And what might the ramifications be for participation and achievement in an information economy? To answer these questions, we turn to classic sociological thinkers, who offer us competing, and at times complementary, explanations for social inequality. Beginning with the conflict perspective, moving on to the cultural perspective, and finishing with the functionalist perspective, we'll explore how three sociological lenses might account for variations in Internet use. Each of these explanations has a particular understanding of the nature of inequality, as it manifests in technology and as it manifests in society at large. We'll use these understandings to situate these digital divides in a larger conversation about American inequality. According to the conflict perspective, which we'll explore in the next chapter, Internet use may be considered part of a middle class and professional skill set. That is, it is something that well-educated and affluent members of society can use to leverage higher wages and more economic power in the capitalist market. The cultural perspective turns our attention to questions of status and lifestyle, framing Internet use as a kind of status marker that sets apart a high status, professional class from a low status, common class. Here, daily Internet use across a broad spectrum of activities constitutes a middle-class lifestyle. Finally, from a functionalist perspective, we might think of the Internet as a mirror of social structure, in which Internet users are rewarded with information and resources. Although this produces inequality, it nurtures a professional class that uses the Internet to advance the needs of society.

In presenting these classic sociological perspectives, we want to suggest that fixing these "digital divides" is not simply a matter of introducing technology and improving Internet access. Rather, it is a question of confronting enduring inequalities in U.S. society. To level the playing field, we can not simply rely on the Internet's potential to increase social interaction, political participation, educational access, and economic activity. We need to understand how the Internet is mapped onto existing inequalities and, in some cases, exacerbates those inequalities. From here, we need to reconfigure the social context in which Internet use takes place. The chapters that follow will not lay out a broad agenda for reconfiguring society along participatory, equal, and inclusive lines, but they will improve our understanding of the ways in which digital technology feeds off a social structure wherein inequality plays a starring role.

Questions for Reading, Reflection, and Debate

1 We began this chapter with an anecdote about a few wired homeless individuals in San Francisco. What is there in the survey data presented in this chapter that would indicate that these individuals are the exception rather than the rule? What are the advantages and disadvantages of relying on anecdotes to explore questions of Internet access and use? If you were to write a more statistically accurate portrayal of Internet use, who would you focus on and why?

2 Revisit the sampling methods used by the Pew Internet &
American Life Project, which we discussed in the introduction to
this chapter and which can be found on the Pew website at
www.pewinternet.org. What population exactly did the project
sample from? Given that this project sought to explore
differences in Internet access and use, do you think it is
problematic that it limited the sample to households with
telephones? Why or why not? What other sampling techniques
might the project explore?

3 The survey data analyzed in this chapter cover a number of years
using a snapshot, or cross-sectional, approach. That is, with each
survey, a different group of individuals is interviewed. An
alternative approach would be to watch the same group of people
over time, what social scientists call a longitudinal approach.
What do you think we could learn differently using a
longitudinal approach? Why do you think the Pew project does
not use a longitudinal approach? If you were to design a
longitudinal study of Internet access and use, what variables or
outcomes would you focus on?

4 The Pew project takes a survey approach to explore Internet use
in American society. Consider more qualitative approaches to
explore this phenomenon. What are the qualitative designs that
you would find most interesting in the study of Internet access
and use? And what kinds of questions would such studies
answer? How would these questions differ from the questions
explored in the survey by Pew?

5 As we saw in this chapter, there are large differences in Internet
use according to education and income. Since education and
income are themselves related—people with higher levels of
education tend to earn more than those with lower levels of
education—some of the effects of income might be due to
education and some of the effects of education might be due to
income. In subsequent chapters, we'll try to disentangle these
effects. For now, think through how education and income might
affect Internet use independently. Concretely, how might higher

levels of education translate into more Internet use? And how might Internet use lead to higher levels of education? Conversely, how might higher levels of income translate into more Internet use? And how might Internet use lead to higher levels of income?

3

INTERNET INEQUALITY FROM A CONFLICT PERSPECTIVE

The bourgeoisie cannot exist without constantly revolutionising the instruments of production, and thereby the relations of production, and with them the whole relations of society. Conservation of the old modes of production in unaltered form was, on the contrary, the first condition of existence for all earlier industrial classes. Constant revolutionising of production, uninterrupted disturbance of all social conditions, everlasting uncertainty and agitation distinguish the bourgeois epoch from all earlier ones. All fixed, fast-frozen relations, with their train of ancient and venerable prejudices and opinions, are swept away, all new-formed ones become antiquated before they can ossify.

—*Karl Marx and Engels* 1978 [1848]

If Karl Marx had been alive to see the dot.com boom, one can imagine him viewing the development as logical, even unsurprising. As Marx and Engels observe in the excerpt from *The Communist Manifesto* above, constant technological and social change is the hallmark of capitalism, which is defined by "everlasting uncertainty and agitation." According to Marx, the capitalist constantly innovates and revolutionizes the productive process in order to maintain power and exploit the working class. Just as it pursues new markets and new methods of management, the capitalist class pursues new technology as a means to maintain its class advantage. In this sense, the Internet and other new forms of technology may be viewed as weapons for the capitalist's arsenal. These weapons are multi-faceted in that they can be used for a variety of purposes. Technology, for example, can be used to create new products and/or to reach out to new consumer markets. Indeed, it seems as if every year, a new technology product becomes the "must have" for mass markets—from iPhones to Blackberries to Wiis. The skills associated with such technology can also be used to establish a market advantage or a market niche. For example, a degree in computer engineering can provide a professional worker with the skills to leverage a higher salary and a higher status in capitalist labor markets.

In addition to understanding the Internet in relation to capitalism, we need to understand the Internet in relation to a changing U.S. economy. Over the past 30 years, the United States has shifted from a goods-producing to a service-producing economy. At this historical moment, the United States has what we might call a post-industrial economy, or a knowledge economy. As a result, industrial jobs are on the decline and service jobs are on the rise, a trend that is expected to continue through 2016. Some of these service jobs are low-skilled (e.g., fast food work); others are high-skilled (e.g., university teaching). But in both cases, skills are central in distinguishing particular social classes. In an industrial economy, capitalists use organizational and technical means to wrestle control over the production process, transforming workers from skilled craftsmen to unskilled cogs in a larger industrial machine. In a post-industrial economy, capitalists have found new organizational and technical means to control and profit from workers. Specifically, they have achieved monopolies over particular forms of knowledge as a way to maintain class advantage.

In this chapter, we'll consider Internet literacy as a particular skill set and knowledge base, the possession of which may be used to maintain class advantage and the lack of which may translate into class disadvantage. From a conflict perspective, knowledge and skills are not distributed equally in society. Even with the advent of universal education, large segments of the population are denied particular forms of knowledge and particular skill sets. As studies have shown, the extreme variation in school quality and the different approaches to discipline and learning mean that some children are channeled into an unskilled working class or a deeply impoverished underclass. Rather than equalizing class relations, then, universal education plays a role in reproducing class inequality. Internet access may act similarly, reproducing social cleavages even while we celebrate its equalizing potential. Without the development of actual Internet competencies, access to the Internet may not lead to a level playing field, and may in fact veil enduring social inequalities. In this chapter, we'll consider these possibilities by examining the conflict perspective in depth, using data from the Pew Internet & American Life Project to explore the relationship between Internet access, technology use, and class advantage.

Class Inequality and Internet Use

According to Karl Marx, two distinct and opposing classes emerge under capitalism: the bourgeoisie, or capitalist class, and the proletariat, or working class. Capitalists are defined by their ownership of the means of production, which is generally understood to mean the tools, technology, and infrastructure associated with production. Lacking such ownership, workers rely on the sale of their labor power. In Marx's theory of surplus value, capitalists extract profit from workers by paying workers less than the value of their labor. Specifically, the capitalist is able to increase the productivity of workers through tools, technology, and other means of production. As a result, workers produce more for the same wage rate. The difference in what workers are paid and the extra value-added to their labor is known as "surplus labor." Through improvements in and control over the production process, capitalists are able to siphon off the extra value that increased productivity provides, allowing for profit accumulation. In the words of Marx: "the capitalist who applies the improved method of production, appropriates to surplus-labor a greater portion of the working-day, than the other capitalists in the same trade" (Marx 1978 [1867], p. 382). Class relations, then, are rooted in the position that each class occupies in the realm of production.

Marx emphasizes that the strategic use of technology is targeted and not indiscriminate. In other words, technology is not employed to address shortages of labor, but rather to decrease the costs of labor.

From this perspective, technology is not neutral or impartial; it specifically and purposefully furthers class interests. The use of capital to enhance productivity has a further implication; it also promotes competition among workers. In *Wage Labor and Capital*, Marx explains: "The greater division of labour enables one worker to do the work of five, ten or twenty; it therefore multiplies competition among the workers twofold, tenfold and twentyfold. The workers do not only compete by selling himself cheaper than another, they compete by one doing the work of five, ten, twenty." At this juncture, Marx argues, tasks are so simplified that work does not require "intense bodily or intellectual faculties." Any unskilled worker can do the job as well as the next (Marx 1978 [1848], pp. 214–15). Without any skill, workers are left with little to no negotiating power in the market. They are replaceable, in a sense lucky to even have a job.

Although Marx recognized a variety of class categories—the bourgeoisie, the petty bourgeoisie, the lumpen proletariat, and so forth—he was most concerned with what he saw as two defining classes under capitalism, namely the capitalist class and the working class. More recent Marxist scholars recognize the importance of other class positions, as well as other dimensions of class power. For example, the Marxist scholar Erik Olin Wright is concerned with the empirical complexities of the middle class, which expanded rapidly throughout the twentieth century, but about which Marx obviously had little to say. To Wright, this class is positioned somewhere between the capitalist and working classes. To the extent that the middle class does not own the means of production, they are exploited in a capitalist sense. But this class may also be considered the exploiter to the extent that it possesses two other valuable assets under capitalism: organizational authority and skill assets. These bases for exploitation are considered secondary to the capitalist form of exploitation. Even so, they constitute another basis for class relations and conflicting interests under capitalism.

What is Wright referring to by "organizational and skill assets"? And what does this have to do with the Internet? Organizational assets generally refer to the possession of authority over others through some high-ranking position in a hierarchy. The classic occupation in which one enjoys organizational authority is management. Skill assets generally refer to the possession of some skill that is valued in the labor market, particularly one that is widely recognized and acknowledged through a credential. The classic occupation in this case would be engineering, wherein one possesses a degree in engineering that is recognized by employers and clients and entitles the engineer to power in workplace decision-making. In this chapter, we are concerned with skill assets, which provide certain workers a more privileged position vis-à-vis unskilled workers.

Wright argues, quite controversially, that the possession of skills or credentials is exploitative of unskilled workers. In Marxian language, ownership of skills allows some workers to appropriate some of the surplus value of others' labor. In more concrete terms, workers with some recognized expertise or knowledge are paid better than workers lacking this expertise or knowledge. And they are paid better because unskilled workers are paid less. Regardless of whether the possession of skills may be understood as a form of exploitation, Wright's idea of skill assets serves us well in a class analysis of the Internet. If we conceptualize Internet use and competencies as a kind of valuable skill set, we can test whether ownership of these skills is associated with a more privileged position in the American socio-economic hierarchy.[1] Does the possession of Internet skills constitute the basis of a more privileged group of workers? Conversely, does the lack of such skills constitute an under-privileged position in the labor market?

The Marxist perspective not only demonstrates how class power is produced, it demonstrates how such power is *reproduced* across generations. From one generation to the next, class advantage is passed on in such a way that children inherit the class position of their parent. Reproducing class privilege not only helps determine the life chances of individuals in capitalist societies, but ensures "the ability of whole social systems to keep going" (Himmelweit 1991, p. 197). The classes are reproduced, as are the essential relationships of exploitation and inequality between the classes. Because the means and processes of production change over time, reproduction does not imply an exact replication of class relationships from one generation to the next:

"Reproduction thus can, and usually does, involve change as well as continuity" (Himmelweit 1991, p. 199). Even so, relative class positions are remarkably stable across generations.

The idea that class positions remain stable across generations is, of course, antithetical to popular thinking in U.S. society. Most people assume that individuals can improve their lives and achieve upward mobility through hard work and smart choices. In this regard, the educational system is seen by many as an avenue toward upward mobility and improvement in class position. Most Marxist scholars, however, view the educational system as an institution that reinforces class disadvantage, rather than as a means toward overcoming that disadvantage. Marxist philosopher Louis Althusser, for example, argued that some states maintain power by controlling the minds of a particular population. One of the primary ways that states do so is through the educational system: "the obligatory (and not least, free) audience of the totality of the children in the capitalist social formation, eight hours a day for five or six days out of seven" allows for a complete indoctrination into a particular state system (Althusser 1971, p. 156).

Samuel Bowles and Herbert Gintis take a similarly critical view of education in their 1976 book, *Schooling in Capitalist America*. The centerpiece of this book is the "correspondence principle," which states that the internal organization of schools corresponds to the organization of the capitalist economic order. According to this principle, students are socialized by the school system to work within the parameters of a competitive capitalist economy and to take on particular positions in that economy. Not only are poor and working-class students denied equal educational opportunities, but they are taught to behave in particular ways and to have particular attitudes that will ensure their submission to managers and employers later in life. Far from ensuring these students' capacity for critical reasoning and/or their mobility in a market economy, the educational system clinches their working-class fate. Writing some 25 years later, Bowles and Gintis (2002) find much historical evidence to support their earlier claims and to continue viewing the educational system as a tool to reproduce class inequality.[2]

To Bowles and Gintis, the purpose of education is to ready a new generation of workers to perform competently, but submissively, in a market economy. Writing in the 1970s, Pierre Bourdieu struck a very similar chord:

> Surely, among all the solutions put forth throughout history to the problem of the transmission of power and privileges, there does not exist one that is better concealed and therefore better adapted to societies ... than that solution which the educational system provides by contributing to the reproduction of the class structure of class relations and by concealing, under an apparently neutral attitude, the fact that it fulfills this function. (Bourdieu and Passeron 1977, p. 178)

Bourdieu's work is particularly significant because of the emphasis he gave to the concept of cultural capital. For Bourdieu, cultural capital exists in three forms: *embodied* ("long-lasting dispositions of the mind and body"), *objectified* ("pictures, books, dictionaries, instruments, machines") and *institutionalized* (educational qualifications) (Bourdieu 1986, p. 47). It is through the unequal distribution of cultural capital that the "unequal scholastic achievements of children originating from the different social classes" may be explained (Bourdieu 1986, p. 47).

Later "resistance theorists" like Willis (1977), Giroux (1983), and Miron (1996) showed how individuals challenged and accommodated this system of reproduction. As they demonstrated, not all students accepted the hidden agenda of education passively; they rebelled against teachers and rejected disciplinary schemas. Though these examples demonstrate ways in which students from lower-class backgrounds contest the socialization that occurs in schools, they do not suggest wholesale disruption of the educational system. Challenges to the status quo (e.g., young men valuing manual labor as masculine over mental labor as feminine) give children from working-class backgrounds a sense of control, but they also consign them to the same working-class positions held by their parents. Occasional success on the part of those from under-privileged backgrounds, not to mention the occupational failure of a son/daughter of privilege, serve to legitimate the process as a whole. Indeed, as Jay MacLeod suggests in *Ain't No Making It: Aspirations and Attainment in a Low-Income Neighborhood*:

> In terms of the immediate perpetuation of class inequality, it matters little how lower-class teenagers respond to the vicissitudes of their situations. No matter how clearly they understand their lives, no matter what cultural innovations they produce, no matter how diligently they devote themselves to school, they cannot escape the constraints of social class. (MacLeod 1995, p. 148)

The literature on education and its role in perpetuating class relations and inequalities informs our analysis of the Internet. To begin, the Internet has become a central part of the U.S. educational system. In 2004, the U.S. Department of Education was hard-pressed to find a school without Internet access (U.S. Department of Education, *Internet Access in U.S. Public Schools and Classrooms: 1994–2005—Table 413*, prepared July 2007). Indeed, as Table 3.1 indicates, Internet access is now available in most schools, both those in high-poverty areas and those in low-poverty areas. Table 3.1 also shows that the number of students sharing a computer connected to the Internet has converged for schools with the least and most disadvantaged student population. As of 2005, there were about four students per computer in both types of schools, compared with 1998, when 10.6 students were sharing computers in relatively well-off schools and 16.8 students were sharing computers in disadvantaged schools.

As the research on education and class inequality suggests, however, we should be wary of reading too much into the spread of Internet access. Increased access may or may not bring about a change in class structure. And, if Internet access mirrors overall trends in education, it is unlikely to change the fundamental features of class inequality. Universal public education certainly has not led to equal educational opportunities or equal economic positions, quite the contrary, according to Marxist scholars. Therefore, we should not expect Internet access to affect socio-economic outcomes dramatically in young adults from

Table 3.1 Public Schools with Internet Access and Student-to-Computer Ratios, 1994–2005

	PERCENT OF STUDENTS ELIGIBLE FOR FREE OR REDUCED-PRICE LUNCH			
	LESS THAN 35 PERCENT	35 TO 49 PERCENT	50 TO 74 PERCENT	75 PERCENT OR MORE
PERCENT OF SCHOOLS WITH INTERNET ACCESS				
1994	39	35	32	18
1995	60	48	41	31
1996	74	59	53	53
1997	86	81	71	62
1998	92	93	88	79
1999	95	98	96	89
2000	99	99	97	94
2001	99	100	99	97
2002	98	100	100	99
2003	100	100	100	99
2005	99	100	100	99
STUDENTS PER INSTRUCTIONAL COMPUTER WITH INTERNET ACCESS				
1998	10.6	10.9	15.8	16.8
1999	7.6	9.0	10.0	16.8
2000	6.0	6.3	7.2	9.1
2001	4.9	5.2	5.6	6.8
2002	4.6	4.5	4.7	5.5
2003	4.2	4.4	4.4	5.1
2005	3.8	3.4	3.6	4.0

Source: U.S. Department of Education, *Internet Access in U.S. Public Schools and Classrooms: 1994–2005—Table 413*, prepared July 2007.

different class backgrounds. Moreover, bundling Internet access into the educational system may not confer the same market advantage to all young people. If students are socialized into different occupational roles in the educational system more generally, it may be that young adults learn to use the Internet in different ways, which correspond to different class positions later in life.

Drawing from the conflict perspective, we would expect to see some relationship between Internet use, particularly Internet use on the job, and class position.[3] In this case, Internet literacy has a kind of market return, with Internet skills leading to greater earnings and higher class positions. We would also expect to see some relationship between class background and Internet use, since conflict theorists argue that

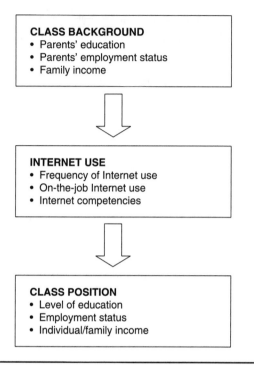

Figure 3.1 Model for the conflict perspective.

class inequality is reproduced across generations. In this case, one's class background helps determine whether one uses the Internet and, if so, for what purpose. Figure 3.1 represents the theoretical model from a conflict perspective, illustrating two relations—one between class background and Internet use, another between Internet use and class position—which we'll test empirically in the next section.

Internet Skills as Class Assets

To test the relationship between class background, Internet use, and class position, we'll use data from the Pew Internet & American Life Project. There are some limitations to using an existing data set to test these relationships. First and foremost, these data were collected with different research questions in mind. In the ideal research situation, data would be collected in a fashion designed to test specific theoretical questions. The research design would likely take an experimental or longitudinal approach so that issues of causality, and not just correlation, could be addressed. As well, the units of analysis, variables, and means of measurement would cleanly operationalize the relevant theoretical concepts. As you can imagine, research strategies of the ideal type are expensive. More typically, researchers use existing data sets and accept that the variables won't match exactly the concepts they're trying to measure.

In our case, we'll be looking at class background, class position, and Internet use using the measurements developed as part of the Pew survey. The Pew survey collected information on parents' education, parents' employment status, and family income, which we'll use to measure class background. The survey also collected information on respondents' employment status and respondents' education, which we'll use to measure class position. The Pew survey did not ask about respondents' income, but we can use family income instead as an income-related measure of class position. For Internet use, the Pew survey asked about on-the-job Internet use, Internet competencies, and frequency of Internet use, all of which we'll use as measures of Internet use. The Pew survey asked a handful of questions that we'll employ to explore further the relationship between family background and Internet use (e.g., whether parents help children do things online).

In the preceding section, we explored the work of Erik Olin Wright, a contemporary Marxist sociologist who offers a broad, comprehensive reformulation of Marx's theories. According to Wright, three types of exploitation, each based on a specific type of asset, coexist and together define the class structure. First, Wright reaffirms the fundamental Marxist distinction between those who own the means of production and those who do not. Wright then goes on to identify two dimensions of stratification that further divide workers: whether or not they possess organizational assets or skill assets. Building on this notion, Internet use and skills may be seen as a type of skill asset that confers power and advantage for those who possess these skills and use them on the job. Exploitation of this asset should yield income rewards for those who employ the Internet at work. Table 3.2 uses the Pew data from 2000 and 2005 to consider the relationship between use of the Internet

Table 3.2 Use of the Internet at Work by Family Income, 2000 and 2005

	2000 PEW SAMPLE[1]			2005 PEW SAMPLE[2]		
	WENT ONLINE YESTERDAY (%)	GO ONLINE, BUT NOT YESTERDAY (%)	DON'T GO ONLINE AT WORK (%)	WENT ONLINE YESTERDAY (%)	GO ONLINE, BUT NOT YESTERDAY (%)	DON'T GO ONLINE AT WORK (%)
Under $10,000	6.3	4.0	89.8	5.7	8.2	86.1
$10,000–$20,000	7.3	7.3	85.4	10.2	16.9	72.9
$20,000–$30,000	12.6	9.6	77.8	15.0	22.0	63.0
$30,000–$40,000	14.2	13.5	72.3	15.3	17.3	67.5
$40,000–$50,000	19.5	14.5	66.0	21.2	38.1	40.8
$50,000–$75,000	19.0	21.5	59.5	33.3	19.5	47.2
$75,000–$100,000	30.6	20.6	48.9	35.6	28.3	36.1
$100,000 or more	27.9	33.3	38.3	46.0	33.7	20.3
Sample size	355	332	1,260	302	271	503

Notes:
1 χ^2 = 192.21 with 14 degrees of freedom, $p < 0.001$.
2 χ^2 = 169.48 with 14 degrees of freedom, $p < 0.001$.

on the job and income. The results distinguish between those who used the Internet at work yesterday and those who ever go online at work.[4]

Looking first at the left-hand side of Table 3.2, employed individuals in families with higher levels of income were far more likely to go online at work in 2000 than those individuals in families with lower levels of income.[5] This relationship is strong and statistically significant. Indeed, the majority of individuals in the low-income families—90 percent of employed individuals in families with incomes below $10,000 and 85 percent in families with incomes between $10,000 and $20,000—never went online at work in 2000. In contrast, a minority of individuals in high-income families—49 percent of employed individuals in families with incomes between $75,000 and $100,000 and 38 percent in families earning in excess of $100,000—did not ever go online at work that year. Moving to the right-hand side of Table 3.2, we see how surprisingly little changed for those at the low end of the income distribution by 2005. Of individuals in families earning under $10,000 per year and between $10,000 and $20,000 per year, 86 and 73 percent never went online at work in 2005, respectively. By contrast, of individuals in families earning over $100,000, 20 percent never went online at work that year.

To explore this issue further, let's consider how use of the Internet at work differs by occupation. We'll use the U.S. Bureau of Labor Statistics' Current Population Survey (CPS) results from October 2003 (Bureau of Labor Statistics 2005). Table 3.3 summarizes the CPS data, which indicate large differences in the use of the Internet by occupation. Management, professional, business and financial operations, and related occupations show the highest levels of Internet use at work.

Table 3.3 Use of the Internet at Work by Occupation, 2003 (Totals in Thousands)

OCCUPATION	TOTAL EMPLOYED	USED THE INTERNET AT WORK	
		NUMBER OF WORKERS	PERCENT OF EMPLOYED
Total, 16 years and over	138,823	57,892	41.7
Management, professional, and related occupations	48,252	32,391	67.1
Management, business, and financial operations occupations	19,600	13,938	71.1
Professional and related occupations	28,652	18,452	64.4
Service occupations	21,887	3,490	15.9
Sales and office occupations	35,492	16,990	47.9
Sales and related occupations	16,051	6,949	43.3
Office and administrative support occupations	19,441	10,041	51.6
Natural resources, construction, and maintenance occupations	15,053	2,497	16.6
Farming, fishing, and forestry occupations	1,270	79	6.3
Construction and extraction occupations	8,392	1,046	12.5
Installation, maintenance, and repair occupations	5,341	1,371	25.7
Production, transportation, and material moving occupations	18,189	2,525	13.9
Production occupations	9,736	1,577	16.2
Transportation and material moving occupations	8,454	948	11.2

Source: Bureau of Labor Statistics 2005.

Next are sales, office, and administrative support occupations, wherein nearly half of all individuals (47 percent) use the Internet on the job. Particularly low levels of on-the-job Internet use are found among farming, fishing, and forestry occupations (6 percent), transportation and material moving occupations (11 percent), and construction and extraction occupations (13 percent). Income data collected by the CPS, however, suggests that a high proportion of Internet use in an occupation does not necessarily confer an income advantage (Bureau of Labor Statistics 2003). For example, more than half (52 percent) of those in office and administrative support occupations report using the Internet at work, but the average annual income for this occupation is $28,540. One-quarter as many workers in construction and extraction industries say they use the Internet at work (13 percent), but their average annual earnings are $37,000. In these two cases, on-the-job Internet use does not equate with higher wages.

The CPS results rely on aggregated data, demonstrating trends in Internet use by occupation rather than by individual. As such, these results do not address whether there are individual level rewards to using the Internet at work. For this purpose, we return to the Pew data. Table 3.4 uses data collected in 2002.[6] Across all occupations, those who used the Internet at work earned significantly more ($47,228) than those who did not use the Internet at work ($39,497).[7] Within specific occupations, use of the Internet at work also conferred an income advantage. Among professional workers, managers, clerical workers, sales workers, service workers, and semi-skilled workers, those who used the Internet at work earned significantly more than those who did not. Only among business owners, manufacturer's representatives, and military/government workers did those who used the Internet have lower average family incomes than those who did not use the Internet at work. Not only are these relatively small occupational groups, totaling about 5 percent of the workforce, but these differences are not statistically significant.

The Pew study includes a variable that combines respondents' number of years using the Internet and the frequency with which they currently use the Internet to classify the population into Internet user

Table 3.4 Use of the Internet at Work and Family Income by Occupation, 2002

OCCUPATION	PERCENT OF WORKFORCE	USE INTERNET AT WORK?[1]		AVERAGE FAMILY INCOME	
		YES (%)	NO (%)	USE INTERNET AT WORK	DON'T USE INTERNET AT WORK
Professional worker	25.0	64.8	35.2	$49,588	$40,861**
Manager, executive, or official	9.7	59.5	40.5	$47,768	$38,357**
Business owner (with 2 or more employees)	2.6	38.7	61.3	$37,469	$42,010
Clerical or office worker	9.0	58.1	41.9	$46,330	$36,540**
Sales worker	6.8	36.8	63.2	$42,767	$33,053**
Manufacturer's representative	1.5	40.8	59.2	$35,550	$44,675
Service worker	13.9	19.4	80.6	$46,170	$34,415**
Skilled trade or craft	12.2	24.7	75.3	$44,747	$43,440
Semi-skilled worker	5.7	14.5	85.5	$46,756	$36,835**
Laborer	8.7	11.4	88.6	$42,087	$37,016
Other	4.1	38.1	61.9	$41,309	$37,969
Military/govt. worker	0.9	67.4	32.6	$43,380	$45,920
Overall	100.0	41.0	59.0	$47,228	$39,497**
Sample size		1,052	1,214	928	1,019

Notes:
1 χ^2 = 395.25 with 11 degrees of freedom, $p < 0.001$.
** T-test of estimated mean difference in income between those using the Internet at work and those not is statistically significant with $p < 0.01$.

types. These user types include "non users," "novices," "mid-range users," "heavy users," and "heaviest users." Among employed individuals in 2005, 23 percent were "non users," 5 percent were "novices," 4 percent were "mid-range users," 50 percent were "heavy users," and 19 percent were "heaviest users." Figure 3.2 shows how the distribution of user types falls according to reported family income. Among employed individuals with a reported family income under $20,000, fewer than half were heavy or heaviest users. Among employed individuals with family incomes of $50,000 or more, at least three-quarters were heavy or heaviest users. Among those with family incomes of $100,000 or more, fully 90 percent were heavy or heaviest users. In Chapter 2, we showed that Internet use among all adults increased with family income; Figure 3.2 demonstrates that this finding is particularly strong among working adults and that it extends beyond mere use of the Internet to include intensity of use. In both instances, the available data are insufficient to claim causality. But combined with Table 3.4, Figure 3.2 suggests a relationship between Internet use and income, the latter of which we are using as a proxy for class position.

These findings provide some evidence that there are income returns to using the Internet at work and that the heaviest Internet users are

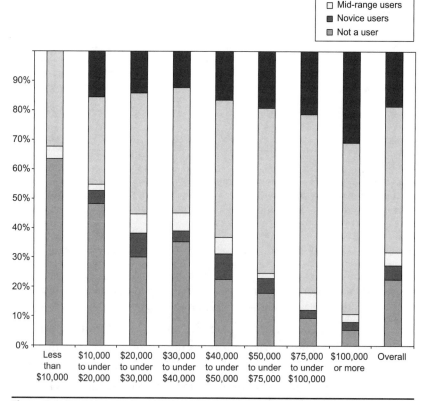

Figure 3.2 Family income of employed american adults by type of Internet user, 2005.

disproportionately found among high-income families. Using the Pew data, let's consider if income differences are linked to possession of particular Internet skills. Table 3.5 summarizes results from a 2005 Pew survey that asked respondents about four particular Internet skills: knowing how to print web pages or other online documents, knowing how to use an online search engine, knowing how to open an

Table 3.5 Internet Skills of American Adults by Employment Status and Educational Level, 2005

EMPLOYED INDIVIDUALS WHO KNOW HOW TO . . .

	PRINT WEBPAGE/ ONLINE INFO (%)	USE ONLINE SEARCH ENGINE (%)	OPEN AN ATTACHMENT (%)	UPLOAD IMAGES/ FILES TO A WEBSITE (%)
Less than high school degree	37.1[1]	39.2[2]	34.0[3]	27.1[4]
High school graduate	47.0	57.4	50.4	30.1
Some college	79.2	84.6	79.9	51.3
Bachelor's degree or higher	87.0	89.9	88.8	55.4

NOT EMPLOYED INDIVIDUALS WHO KNOW HOW TO . . .

	PRINT WEBPAGE/ ONLINE INFO (%)	USE ONLINE SEARCH ENGINE (%)	OPEN AN ATTACHMENT (%)	UPLOAD IMAGES/ FILES TO A WEBSITE (%)
Less than high school degree	16.1[5]	18.9[6]	16.3[7]	11.3[8]
High school graduate	27.1	32.6	28.0	16.1
Some college	45.2	53.8	47.8	25.7
Bachelor's degree or higher	58.3	63.6	62.6	33.5

Notes:
1 $N = 1,269, \chi^2 = 207.14, p < 0.001.$
2 $N = 1,271, \chi^2 = 181.12, p < 0.001.$
3 $N = 1,271, \chi^2 = 207.23, p < 0.001.$
4 $N = 1,266, \chi^2 = 162.14, p < 0.001$
5 $N = 905, \chi^2 = 110.67, p < 0.001.$
6 $N = 904, \chi^2 = 105.72, p < 0.001.$
7 $N = 897, \chi^2 = 112.97, p < 0.001.$
8 $N = 902, \chi^2 = 107.17, p < 0.001.$

attachment, and knowing how to upload images or files to a website. In the upper panel of this exhibit, the percentage of employed adults able to do each of these tasks without any assistance is reported for each level of education. Here we see a significant and strong relationship between education and Internet skills, with employed adults with higher levels of education more capable of all four tasks than those with lower levels of education. In each case, the percentage of employed persons with a bachelor's degree who can do the task is more than double the percentage of employed persons with less than a high school degree who can do the task.

The lower panel of Table 3.5 provides comparable results for those who were not employed when they were interviewed in 2005. At all levels of education, and for all of the tasks considered, we see significantly lower levels of competency among those not employed compared to those employed in the same educational category. Moreover, among those not employed, the gap between those with the lowest and highest levels of education is even greater. For each task, the percentage of unemployed persons with a bachelor's degree who can do the task without any help is more than triple the percentage of unemployed persons with less than a high school degree who can do the task without help.

A similar analysis is presented in Table 3.6. In this instance, the focus is on family income rather than educational background. Here, the relationship is similar to that shown in Table 3.5: those with higher family incomes are more likely to have the skills to do each task without help than those with lower family incomes. The gap is even greater when we consider those who were not employed at the time of their interview. Without more detailed data on how individuals use these Internet skills on the job, we can not conclude that Internet skills lead to higher incomes. Indeed, the fact that the Internet skills gap is greater among the unemployed suggests that individuals are not necessarily rewarded in the labor market for their Internet skill set. Rather, these results suggest a certain level of Internet competency comes with education, indicating that general Internet savvy is a form of cultural capital. Internet skills such as knowing how to use a search engine or

Table 3.6 Internet Skills of American Adults by Employment Status and Familiy Income, 2005

EMPLOYED INDIVIDUALS WHO KNOW HOW TO . . .

	PRINT WEBPAGE/ ONLINE INFO (%)	USE ONLINE SEARCH ENGINE (%)	OPEN AN ATTACHMENT (%)	UPLOAD IMAGES/ FILES TO A WEBSITE (%)
Less than $10,000	51.6[1]	50.0[2]	41.9[3]	41.9[4]
$10,000–$20,000	44.4	52.2	48.9	29.0
$20,000–$30,000	53.4	58.6	56.0	40.6
$30,000–$40,000	66.4	69.8	68.3	37.7
$40,000–$50,000	66.8	74.9	67.7	40.3
$50,000–$75,000	73.5	86.0	80.3	43.9
$75,000–$100,000	81.3	85.5	84.0	53.2
$100,000 or more	88.1	92.2	88.7	63.5

NOT EMPLOYED INDIVIDUALS WHO KNOW HOW TO . . .

	PRINT WEBPAGE/ ONLINE INFO (%)	USE ONLINE SEARCH ENGINE (%)	OPEN AN ATTACHMENT (%)	UPLOAD IMAGES/ FILES TO A WEBSITE (%)
Less than $10,000	23.0[5]	24.0[6]	18.0[7]	8.4[8]
$10,000–$20,000	18.6	26.8	21.4	10.0
$20,000–$30,000	26.7	31.8	28.1	18.4
$30,000–$40,000	33.8	44.6	40.3	23.6
$40,000–$50,000	45.8	57.6	55.9	33.9
$50,000–$75,000	64.9	71.4	66.7	35.5
$75,000–$100,000	87.8	85.4	91.7	39.6
$100,000 or more	79.7	84.7	84.7	64.4

Notes:
1 $N = 1,047, \chi^2 = 121.65, p < 0.001.$
2 $N = 1,048, \chi^2 = 126.56, p < 0.001.$
3 $N = 1,048, \chi^2 = 127.02, p < 0.001.$
4 $N = 1,043, \chi^2 = 112.33, p < 0.001.$
5 $N = 605, \chi^2 = 154.49, p < 0.001.$
6 $N = 604, \chi^2 = 139.38, p < 0.001.$
7 $N = 600, \chi^2 = 154.98, p < 0.001.$
8 $N = 603, \chi^2 = 146.44, p < 0.001.$

how to open an attachment may be markers, or indicators, of cultural capital rather than skills that may be marketed for greater income.[8]

As we discussed in the theoretical section of this chapter, the reproduction of an unequal class structure is a key element of the conflict perspective. Thus, we would expect to see Internet class advantage, or disadvantage, passed down from one generation to the next.

Specifically, we would expect that children growing up in families with higher levels of education and income would be more likely to be around adults who use the Internet and in homes where the Internet is available. In 2005, Pew respondents were asked if they had ever helped a child or an adult do something online that they could not do on their own. Turning to Table 3.7, we see that there is a strong statistical relationship between parents' education and whether they had helped a child do something online. Among those parents with less than a high school degree, over half do not even use the Internet and only a little more than 20 percent ever helped a child do something online. Parents with a high school degree were twice as likely to have helped a child do something online; those with at least some college education were more than three times as likely to do so. Table 3.7 also shows that a parent who is employed is slightly more likely to have helped a child. This suggests that employed parents might be drawing on experience and skills acquired on the job.

In Table 3.8, the same analysis is conducted using family income rather than educational achievement. The results are quite similar.

Table 3.7 Parental Assistance in Children's Online Tasks by Parents' Education, 2005

HAVE YOU EVER HELPED A CHILD DO SOMETHING ONLINE THEY COULDN'T DO THEMSELVES?				
	LESS THAN HIGH SCHOOL DEGREE (%)	HIGH SCHOOL GRADUATE (%)	SOME COLLEGE (%)	BACHELOR'S OR HIGHER (%)
ALL PARENTS[1]				
Yes	21.7	42.3	68.2	69.1
No	24.3	22.0	21.0	26.8
Don't go online	55.9	35.7	10.8	4.1
	100.0	100.0	100.0	100.0
EMPLOYED PARENTS[2]				
Yes	25.6	49.4	66.9	69.9
No	26.9	17.6	2.5	26.3
Don't go online	47.4	33.0	10.6	3.8
	100.0	100.0	100.0	100.0

Percentages may not equal 100% due to rounding.
Notes:
1 $N = 673, \chi^2 = 126.53, p < 0.05$.
2 $N = 531, \chi^2 = 79.93, p < 0.01$.

Table 3.8 Parental Assistance in Children's Online Tasks by Family Income, 2005

HAVE YOU EVER HELPED A CHILD DO SOMETHING ONLINE THEY COULDN'T DO THEMSELVES?

	LESS THAN $10,000 (%)	$10,000– $20,000 (%)	$20,000– $30,000 (%)	$30,000– $40,000 (%)	$40,000– $50,000 (%)	$50,000– $75,000 (%)	$75,000– $100,000 (%)	$100,000 OR MORE (%)
ALL PARENTS[1]								
Yes	31.3	31.8	49.3	56.1	51.9	58.9	64.5	72.5
No	24.1	19.6	26.1	17.3	24.1	27.3	28.3	22.0
Don't go online	44.6	48.6	24.6	26.6	24.1	13.9	7.2	5.5
	100.0	100.0	100.0	100.0	100.0	100.0	100.0	100.0
EMPLOYED PARENTS[2]								
Yes	46.2	29.2	47.5	62.2	53.3	59.2	68.0	75.3
No	28.2	15.4	29.7	14.4	26.1	28.3	24.2	20.7
Don't go online	25.6	55.4	22.8	23.4	20.7	12.6	7.8	4.0
	100.0	100.0	100.0	100.0	100.0	100.0	100.0	100.0

Percentages may not equal 100% due to rounding.

Notes:

1 N = 673, χ^2 = 126.53, $p < 0.05$.

2 N = 531, χ^2 = 79.93, $p < 0.01$.

Parents in low-income families go online less frequently and, if they do, are significantly less likely to report that they have ever helped a child do something online. Taken together, these findings suggest that existing patterns of Internet use by American adults have the potential to perpetuate rather than challenge class advantages that parents pass on to their children.

The Pew data permit us to push this analysis further still. In 2004, over 1,000 teenage children of Pew respondents were surveyed as well. These children, ages 12 to 17, were asked about their Internet use and knowledge. These data can be combined with parents' responses to consider questions of Internet use and intergenerational class mobility. Looking at Table 3.9, we see that parents' educational achievement and family income are both significantly related to teenagers' use of the Internet. Approximately three-quarters of teenagers whose parents had less than a high school degree reported going online, compared with over 90 percent of teenagers with a parent who had a bachelor's degree. Table 3.9 also summarizes differences in teenage Internet use according to family income. Here, too, there is significant evidence that the children of well-off parents are more likely to use the Internet than

Table 3.9 Teen Internet Use by Parent's Education and Family Income, 2004

| | DOES A TEENAGER GO ONLINE? | |
	YES (%)	NO (%)
PARENT'S EDUCATION[1]		
Less than high school degree	76.2	23.8
High school graduate	81.2	18.8
Some college	90.4	9.6
Bachelor's degree or higher	93.2	6.8
FAMILY INCOME[2]		
Less than $20,000	65.2	34.8
$20,000–$30,000	82.0	18.0
$30,000–$40,000	87.3	12.7
$40,000–$75,000	87.5	12.5
$75,000 or more	93.1	6.9

Notes:
1 $N = 1,097$, $\chi^2 = 30.92$, $p < 0.001$.
2 $N = 998$, $\chi^2 = 44.526$, $p < 0.001$.

their peers in less privileged families. Whereas our previous findings indicated that education played a stronger role than income, income effects are particularly striking in this instance. Less than two-thirds of teenagers in families with incomes under $20,000 said they went online, compared to over 90 percent of teenagers in families with incomes of $75,000 and higher.

The Pew data also allow us to assess whether parents' education and family income are associated with the online competencies of children. As Table 3.10 shows, there is strong evidence that class advantage is transferred to the next generation in this regard as well. For three online skills—knowing how to print web pages or other online documents,

Table 3.10 Teen Internet Skills by Parent's Education and Family Income, 2004

TEENAGER KNOWS HOW TO . . .	PRINT WEBPAGE/ ONLINE INFO (%)	USE ONLINE SEARCH ENGINE (%)	OPEN AN ATTACHMENT (%)	UPLOAD IMAGES/ FILES TO A WEBSITE (%)
PARENT'S EDUCATION				
Less than high school degree	69.1[1]	68.0[2]	45.7[3]	46.1[4]
High school graduate	76.8	75.1	56.7	46.0
Some college	86.3	82.3	60.5	53.2
Bachelor's degree or higher	89.2	90.0	72.5	46.0
FAMILY INCOME				
Less than $20,000	58.9[5]	53.6[6]	34.1[7]	40.1[8]
$20,000–$30,000	76.3	73.7	50.9	46.3
$30,000–$40,000	84.5	76.7	55.0	42.8
$40,000–$75,000	81.3	82.1	62.9	51.4
$75,000 or more	89.8	89.3	70.3	48.4

Notes:
1 $N = 1,097, \chi^2 = 29.76, p < 0.001$.
2 $N = 1,097, \chi^2 = 33.99, p < 0.001$.
3 $N = 1,084, \chi^2 = 27.07, p < 0.001$.
4 $N = 1,094, \chi^2 = 1.51, p = 0.68$.
5 $N = 998, \chi^2 = 40.28, p < 0.001$.
6 $N = 998, \chi^2 = 51.73, p < 0.001$.
7 $N = 998, \chi^2 = 44.66, p < 0.001$.
8 $N = 987, \chi^2 = 3.63, p = 0.46$.

knowing how to use an online search engine, and knowing how to open an attachment—there are differences of 20 percentage points or more between teenagers whose parents did not finish high school and those whose parents graduated from college. Nearly twice as many teenagers from families with incomes of $75,000 or more knew how to open an attachment than teenagers living in families with incomes under $20,000. Interestingly, the knowledge of how to upload images or files to a website did not vary with parents' educational background or family income, as the lower panel of Table 3.10 shows.

The link between teenagers' Internet use and skills and parental educational background and family income implicates the Internet in the reproduction of class privilege. Teenagers may have acquired Internet experience and knowledge in class-privileged homes, from parents who draw on their own Internet skills. Or they may have acquired Internet experience and knowledge in class-privileged schools, where technology resources are greater due to the larger local tax base. Whatever the source of the Internet advantage—and the source is most likely a combination of home and school—children of parents with higher levels of education and from families with higher income will benefit from this Internet know-how as they transition from school to work since employers now place a premium on Internet skills.

One less obvious aspect of the intergenerational transfer of online competencies is worth noting. The transfer of Internet skills is unlikely to be one-directional. Indeed, data from the Pew project indicate that more teenagers report providing adults with online assistance than vice versa. As we see in Table 3.11, column one, teenagers with parents with lower levels of education and teenagers from lower income families are significantly less likely to report helping an adult with tasks online. It appears here that the parents of disadvantaged children are themselves disadvantaged by the fact that their children are less likely to use the Internet. When we limit our analysis to teenagers who go online (column two), there are no significant differences, suggesting that Internet differences among adults might not be so great if children gained Internet skills and were able to assist their parents in learning this skill set.

Table 3.11 Teen Assistance with Adult's Online Tasks by Parent's Education and Family Income, 2004

PERCENTAGE OF TEENAGERS ASSISTING PARENTS WITH ONLINE TASKS . . .		
	ALL TEENS (%)	TEENS WHO GO ONLINE (%)
PARENT'S EDUCATION		
Less than high school degree	58.4[1]	76.8[3]
High school graduate	68.1	83.8
Some college	73.5	81.2
Bachelor's degree or higher	76.3	81.8
FAMILY INCOME		
Less than $20,000	52.6[2]	80.7[4]
$20,000 to $30,000	62.7	76.1
$30,000 to $40,000	70.0	80.2
$40,000 to $75,000	70.6	80.8
$75,000 or more	78.3	84.1

Notes:
1 $N = 1{,}094$, $\chi^2 = 10.14$, $p < 0.017$.
2 $N = 995$, $\chi^2 = 16.78$, $p = 0.002$.
3 $N = 967$, $\chi^2 = 1.00$, $p = 0.801$.
4 $N = 877$, $\chi^2 = .407$, $p = 0.982$.

Tables 3.12 and 3.13 use 2000 and 2006 Pew data to determine if the patterns of Internet use discussed in Chapter 2 also hold for young adults ages 18 to 24. Looking first at the left-hand side of Table 3.12, we see that ever going online and using the Internet on the previous day varied with level of education in 2000. As was the case among adults, young adults with at least some college experience were far more likely to have ever been online and to have used the Internet on the previous day when compared with young adults with less education. By 2006, this pattern had changed somewhat. By that year, the higher levels of use found among those with at least some college education were no longer statistically significant, indicating that Internet experience had reached a broad level of ubiquity. Even in 2006, however, those with at least some college education were approximately 50 percent more likely to have reported Internet use on the previous day than those with lower levels of education. Thus, daily Internet use appears to vary by education even for the next generation.

Table 3.12 Internet Use Among 18 to 24 Year Old Americans by Education, 2000 and 2006

	2000 PEW SAMPLE		2006 PEW SAMPLE	
	EVER BEEN ONLINE[1] (%)	WENT ONLINE PREVIOUS DAY[2] (%)	EVER BEEN ONLINE[3] (%)	WENT ONLINE PREVIOUS DAY[4] (%)
Less than high school degree	43.9	18.1	85.0	50.2
High school graduate	57.7	23.9	78.1	49.8
Some college	84.3	49.2	94.7	72.5
Bachelor's degree or higher	85.7	39.0	96.9	79.7
Sample size	477	477	279	279

Notes:
1 χ^2 = 56.91 with 3 degrees of freedom, $p < 0.001$.
2 χ^2 = 36.54 with 3 degrees of freedom, $p < 0.001$.
3 χ^2 = 11.33 with 3 degrees of freedom, $p < 0.01$.
4 χ^2 = 18.58 with 3 degrees of freedom, $p < 0.001$.

Table 3.13 Internet Use Among 18 to 24 Year Old Americans by Family Income, 2000 and 2006

	2000 PEW SAMPLE		2006 PEW SAMPLE	
	EVER BEEN ONLINE[1] (%)	WENT ONLINE PREVIOUS DAY[2] (%)	EVER BEEN ONLINE[3] (%)	WENT ONLINE PREVIOUS DAY[4] (%)
Under $10,000	52.2	32.7	75.4	41.5
$10,000–$20,000	40.9	16.2	84.4	39.4
$20,000–$30,000	64.6	36.7	80.4	43.5
$30,000–$40,000	71.3	36.8	88.8	70.4
$40,000–$50,000	81.8	47.8	100.0	86.5
$50,000–$75,000	86.9	31.8	93.8	76.5
$75,000–$100,000	88.1	66.7	93.4	87.0
$100,000 or more	94.6	50.9	96.0	69.7
Sample size	368	368	219	219

Notes:
1 χ^2 = 48.73 with 7 degrees of freedom, $p < 0.001$.
2 χ^2 = 25.50 with 7 degrees of freedom, $p < 0.001$.
3 χ^2 = 10.67 with 7 degrees of freedom, $p = 0.15$.
4 χ^2 = 25.23 with 7 degrees of freedom, $p < 0.001$.

Table 3.13 summarizes a similar analysis, where Internet use patterns of young adults are broken down by family income. In 2000, the relationship between family income and Internet use of young adults was similar to that of the population at large. Under one-third of young adults living in families earning under $20,000 had been online the previous day, compared with over half of young adults in families with incomes of $75,000 and over. By 2006, however, there was no longer a significant relationship between family income and ever having been online. As with education, Internet use on the previous day continued to vary by family income in 2006.

Summary and Conclusion

In this chapter, we focused on two aspects of the conflict perspective that enable us to better understand the link between the Internet and inequality. First, going back to the work of Marx, inequality in a capitalist society rests on the ability of a dominant class to use its assets to maintain an advantage in the productive process. Recent theorists define skill as a kind of asset. In today's information-based economy, Internet access and use can be understood as an asset used to maintain class privilege and power. Second, capitalist relations of production can only be maintained if the inequalities upon which they rest are reproduced from one generation to the next. If Internet access and use are among the critical skill assets that allow for exploitation in today's processes of production, then access to the Internet and possession of Internet skills must be passed on to young people to secure their position in the market economy.

Statistical evidence from the Pew Internet & American Life Project suggests the extent to which Internet use and Internet skills are associated with socio-economic status. The evidence also suggests that this relationship is transferred across generations. Although Internet access is being equalized in schools, there are real, demonstrable differences in the frequency of Internet use and in particular Internet skills among young adults, differences that vary by parents' education and family income. Assuming that parents' education and family income are relatively good indicators of class position, as well as good indicators of school quality, we can say that young adults in under-privileged families and under-privileged school systems do not enjoy *frequent* Internet use and do not have the same Internet know-how.

The analyses presented in this chapter also suggest that there are other influences at work in the relationship between the Internet and inequality. Specifically, there may be a cultural basis for how Internet savvy translates into class power. In the next chapter, we'll consider the work of Max Weber, who provides the foundation for a cultural perspective on economic life and inequality. This perspective will help guide our analysis of the Internet from a less materialistic or deterministic lens. In *The Protestant Ethic and the Spirit of Capitalism*, Weber sought to show a cultural relationship between Protestant religious values and capitalist principles. He also demonstrated how social status, not simply class position, acted to stratify society. This view complemented the work of Marx and other scholars. With this in mind, we now turn to the perspective of cultural sociology to see how it can further our understanding of the digital divide.

Questions for Reading, Reflection, and Debate

1   For Wright, the possession of skill assets affords members of the middle class a privileged class position under capitalism. For these skills to be of value in the labor market, however, they should have some credential attached to them. That is, they need to be recognized formally by the wider society. Consider the ways in which Internet skills are attached to particular credentials or forms of recognition. How do individuals "prove" they possess Internet skills? And how do they market their Internet skills in the larger economy? Is it necessary for these skills to be recognized formally to have an effect on class position or class advantage? Or are there other ways in which Internet skills, lacking formal credentials, might translate into market advantage?

2   In this chapter, we were limited in our measurement of Internet know-how by the questions asked by the Pew survey. For example, we considered four different Internet skills (e.g., how to

open an attachment) as a way to assess Internet competency. If we could design a survey for the purpose of measuring possession of Internet skills, especially those skills that might have some market advantage, what kind of questions would we ask? In other words, what kinds of Internet skills might be most valuable in conferring a market or class advantage? And how might those skills be passed down through families or taught in schools?

3 In their analysis of technological change and skill upgrading, Card and DiNardo (2002) contend that there are short-term wage premiums associated with the possession of technical skills, such that those who possess cutting-edge technical skills enjoy higher earnings for a time. Once the larger population obtains these skills, however, the wage premium declines. What does this finding suggest about the relationship we found between Internet skills and family income? And how might we test Card and DiNardo's finding in relation to Internet skills? Finally, what Internet skills might be in abundant supply and what Internet skills might be in scarce supply in today's U.S. workforce?

4 DiMaggio et al. (2001) cite research showing that low-income and minority students use computers at school as much as their middle-class and white counterparts, but that low-income and minority schools tend to use computer labs as a form of babysitting (p. 43). Likewise, Bolt and Crawford (2000) show that teacher training in Internet technology lags behind the introduction of the Internet into low-income and minority schools, nullifying any advantage that this technology might confer to these students. Thinking through these examples, explore how Internet use may differ in low-income versus middle-class schools, and how these differences may affect how students experience the transition from school to work. Can variation in the way that schools use the Internet be understood as providing some students with the competencies to use the Internet and others the competencies to be used *by* the Internet?

5 In this chapter, we have suggested that Internet competencies and use are related to class position. Indicating a relationship between the two, however, is different from explicating how Internet savvy gets translated into higher earnings. It could be that workers are paid higher wages or salaries on account of their demonstrable Internet skills. It could also be that heavy Internet users are more effective at using the Internet to access information and converting that information into some occupational advantage. Finally, it could be that possession of Internet skills is a proxy for some other attribute that confers advantage to the Internet user. Explore these different interpretations and weigh their validity relative to one another.

4

INTERNET INEQUALITY FROM A CULTURAL PERSPECTIVE

"Classes" are groups of people who, from the standpoint of specific interests, have the same economic position. Ownership or non-ownership of material goods or of definite skills constitute the "class-situation." "Status" is a quality of social honor or a lack of it, and is in the main conditioned as well as expressed through a specific style of life. Social honor can stick directly to a class-situation, and it is also, indeed most of the time, determined by the average class situation of the status-group members. This, however, is not necessarily the case. Status membership, in turn, influences the class-situation in that the style of life required by status groups makes them prefer special kinds of property or gainful pursuits and reject others.

—*Weber* 1946, p. 405

For those of us who routinely go online, the Internet has radically changed the way we communicate and how we interact with others. With the Internet becoming such an important medium of social interaction, those who lack access to the Internet and those whose use of the Internet is limited may be excluded from major channels of communication. Internet-based interaction is conditional upon our being "in the know," as well as the recognition by others that we "belong" to a particular virtual reality. The exclusive nature of the Internet is nowhere more evident than in the case of Facebook, in which our connections to others as "friends" must be recognized by both parties. One can not simply establish "friends" through Facebook; one's invitation to become a "friend" must be accepted by the other person as a form of recognition that we belong to their group and their world. Once we have established someone as a "friend," our access to the details of their daily life becomes a kind of social currency, a way to not simply stay in touch but to confirm our belonging and our membership in a particular group.

Although he did not live during the Facebook era, the kinds of interactions we see on Facebook, and the social inequalities that govern them, were of central concern to another prominent sociological thinker by the name of Max Weber. Like Marx, Weber was concerned with differences in class position. But he made a distinction between "class" and what he called "status." To Weber, these two sources of inequality are related, but distinct.[1] Class position is defined with reference to markets and the ownership of property or skills. Status positions are marked by distinctive views of the world and styles of life (Weber 1946, p. 187). Aspiration and adoption of these lifestyles are not enough to warrant inclusion in a particular status position. Others in a status group must acknowledge the individual as being part of the collective, particularly through reciprocal social interactions and a recognized sense of belonging. Thus, for Weber, status rests on social acceptance and group closure. Just as there are different bases for class position, so too are there different sources of status—membership in the right club, living in the right neighborhood, and being invited to the right parties. Our access to these privileges affords us more or less social prestige, which, in turn, determines our status position. Combined with class distinctions, these status differentials yield a rich and complex stratification system associated with differences in life chances and lifestyles.

The cultural perspective, with its roots in the sociology of Max Weber, turns our attention to the multi-dimensional nature of inequality. It also raises the issue of lifestyle and consumption, which become critical angles to evaluate the impact of new forms of information and communication technology. Finally, this perspective raises the importance of occupations and families in determining our access to and use of the Internet, since prestige is often associated with our occupations and status is often passed down through families. After reviewing the major ideas of the cultural perspective, we will return to the Pew data to explore the relationship between occupational status, family background, and Internet use. In doing so, we'll consider the extent to which the Internet may be viewed as a feature of middle-class and upper middle-class life conduct, as well as a cultural boundary marking the class divide.

Status Inequality and Internet Use

Like Marx, Weber appreciated the importance of one's class position and its relation to broader economic forces. Weber believed that one could speak of a class when a group of people shared a "specific causal component of their life chances." And he understood that causal component as being defined by the possession of goods and opportunities for income that had a market value (Weber 1946, p. 181). In this view, classes are groups of people situated similarly in relation to commodity or labor markets on account of their possession of capital or skills. Because they are situated similarly, individuals with the same class situation are likely to have the same chances in life. From here, though, Weber departs from Marx, depicting inequality along dimensions other than class. In particular, Weber distinguished class from status, the latter reflecting stratification according to lifestyle and consumption. Specifically, restrictions on social interaction set status group members apart from non-members, stratifying society along social lines, often with material consequences. According to Weber, status stratification rested on honor, or prestige, rather than on economic assets. Because status distinctions are not determined by the logic of the market, Weber understood them to be a hindrance to the free development of markets. Whereas "the market 'knows no personal distinctions'," Weber argued, "the status order means precisely the reverse" (Weber 1946, p. 192).

Once established, status distinctions translate into particular lifestyles and forms of life conduct. In explicating the relation between status and lifestyle, the work of German sociologist Ralf Dahrendorf is considered classic. In *Society and Democracy in Germany* (1967), Dahrendorf draws from the cultural perspective to define class as the lens an individual uses to view the world in which he or she acts. Class, here, is not simply a structural position with relation to markets, but a shared perspective that defines and enables patterns of social interaction among individuals with a common class background. Dahrendorf disputed the common belief that in postwar Germany the working class had become so fragmented that it no longer made sense to speak of it as a class. While granting that there were important differences between workers (e.g., skilled versus unskilled), Dahrendorf maintained that there was still a common working-class *culture*. The evidence he marshaled to support this view was decidedly Weberian: the working class was unified in terms of lifestyle choices, values, and attitudes.

The range of phenomena that fall under lifestyles and life conduct is considerable. From the clothes we wear and the cars we drive, to the medical and dental care we receive, we live in ways that are distinct from or similar to others depending on our status position. The schools our children attend and the spouses they choose are also correlated with status position. Indeed, Abel and Cockerham (1993) argue that the breadth of phenomena implied by Weber is underestimated by many social scientists who take a cultural perspective. They believe Weber's concept of *Lebensführung* was inappropriately translated as "lifestyle" in the two major English-language translations of Weber's work. As a result, Weber's two distinct terms *Lebensführung* (life conduct) and *Lebensstil* (lifestyles) were given the same imprecise meaning "lifestyle." Life conduct goes beyond one's friendship networks and neighborhood of residence to encompass personal choices and individual behavior. Thus, we may aspire to become president, or spend our Friday night at a bowling alley, or use a payday lender depending on our status. And this implicates the Internet in important ways, since Internet use represents a form of individual behavior and since Internet resources may facilitate interaction among members of particular status groups.

For Weberians, two factors play an especially important role in distinguishing one's status position and, hence, one's lifestyle choices:

family background and occupational group. Both confer different levels of prestige or honor. Research has been particularly robust on the prestige (or lack thereof) that occupations provide individuals. Although occupations may be defined in class terms, they may also be defined in terms of status, especially when, in their efforts to gain market advantage, members of an occupation follow a strategy of closure. Using mechanisms like licensing and certification, many occupational groups restrict access to the occupation and attempt to secure monetary and non-monetary rewards greater than they would obtain in an unrestricted market. Indeed, recent work on occupations from a cultural perspective has sought to remind readers of the difference between class and occupation. Hogan (2005), for example, explains: "Class (e.g., employer) is a work relationship rooted in exploitation at the firm level. Occupation (e.g., physician) is a status rooted in opportunity hoarding at the national level" (p. 655). Thus, occupations confer a level of prestige independent of wage or salary, such that the most prestigious occupations are not necessarily the highest paid occupations (e.g., teachers and firefighters).

We have seen that the cultural perspective views inequality as multi-dimensional. Accordingly, differences in Internet use should be related to class position, but also status differences, or differences in occupational prestige and family background. To the extent that the Internet is associated with prestige and status, individuals in high-prestige occupations and individuals from prestigious families should be more likely to use the Internet, especially on a daily basis. These effects should be *independent* of class differences, understood here as education and income. In addition, if status implicates consumption and lifestyle, then we should see high status individuals using the Internet across a variety of domains—in consumption as well as production, and for purposes of communication as well as information. Figure 4.1 depicts the theoretical model from a cultural perspective, illustrating the related, but independent, effects of social class and social status on Internet lifestyles.

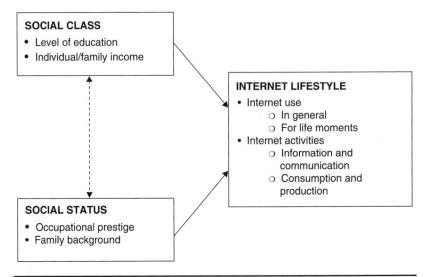

Figure 4.1 Model for the cultural perspective.

Internet Use as Status and Lifestyle

Based on the preceding summary of the cultural perspective and its relation to the Internet, let's consider the empirical evidence. Table 4.1 provides the results from a multivariate analysis of factors related to the use of the Internet. Multivariate logistic regression is a commonly used statistical technique that assesses the independent impact of a variety of factors on a binary outcome variable. By "binary outcome variable," we mean whether an outcome occurs or not. In this case, the outcome variable is whether a person uses the Internet or not. Regression estimates the odds that this outcome will occur. We'll begin by using some basic demographic variables to see how they independently affect the odds that an individual used the Internet on the day prior to his or her interview. We're especially concerned with Internet use on the previous day because this suggests daily Internet use, or an everyday lifestyle that involves use of the Internet.

The results in column [1] of Table 4.1 are based on a very simple demographic model that uses gender, age, and race to predict whether or not an individual used the Internet on the previous day.[2] From here,

Table 4.1 Effects of Demographic Characteristics and Class Variables on Odds of Going Online the Previous Day, 2006

	MODEL [1]	MODEL [2]
CONSTANT		0.69*
Female: Male	1.12**	1.01
Black: White and Others	0.47**	0.77
Asian: White and Others	1.99*	2.04
Age 65 and older: Age 18–44 years	0.17**	0.29**
Age 45–64 years: Age 18–44 years	0.64**	0.57**
Less than high school degree: Some college or more		0.27**
High school degree: Some college or more		0.42**
Not employed: Employed full or part-time		0.73*
Retired or disabled: Employed full or part-time		0.61**
Family income		1.30**
Nagelkerke Pseudo R2	0.15	0.31
Sample size	3,914	3,092

Source: Pew Internet & American Life Survey, March 2006.
Note:
** $p < 0.01$.

we'll add independent variables that relate to social class, namely level of education, employment status, and income. The results of the regression model combining our demographic and class variables may be found in column [2] of Table 4.1.

The purely demographic analysis presented as Model [1] is not unlike the univariate demographic results presented in Chapter 2. Blacks are less likely than non-blacks to have used the Internet on the previous day; Asians are more likely than non-Asians to have done so; and older adults are less likely than younger adults to have done so. The effects of race and age found in Chapter 2 are unchanged when gender, age, and race are all considered at once. The one important difference between these multivariate results and the univariate results from Chapter 2 is that once race and age differences are taken into account, women are significantly more likely to have used the Internet on the previous day than men.

The story becomes more interesting when education, employment, and income are added to the model. As we've already seen, those with at least some college education are significantly more likely to have gone online the previous day than those with a high school degree or less. The employed are more likely to have gone online than those not employed. And income significantly increases the odds that an individual went online the day prior to being interviewed. None of this changes when these factors are all considered simultaneously. Furthermore, the age effects persist, with those over the age of 44, and especially those 65 and older, less likely to have gone online on the previous day. Interestingly, the effects of gender and race *lose* their statistical significance in Model [2]. That is, once education, employment, and income are taken into account, the odds of an individual having gone online the previous day are unaffected by gender and race. It is not variation in gender and race that accounts for differences in daily Internet use, then, but variation in education, employment, and income, all of which are correlated with race and gender. Even the age effects that persist in Model [2] may well be proxies for the differing educational and employment experiences of those over the age of 44.

We may interpret these results as suggesting that class differences are critical to differences in daily Internet use, which the Weberian perspective would predict. But what about status differences, which this perspective also emphasizes? As noted in the previous section, the cultural perspective uses occupational prestige as an indicator of social status. Data from the Pew Internet & American Life Project, however, lacks sufficient detail on occupations and occupational prestige. Therefore, we'll use another relevant source of data: the 2004 General Social Survey (GSS). The 2004 GSS survey includes precise industry and occupational data for each respondent's current or most recent job. Occupational data were coded using U.S. Census categories, which were then associated with prestige scores from the widely used NORC/GSS Occupational Prestige Scale (GSS Methodological Reports No. 69 and 70). These scores range from 17 to 86, with higher scores signifying higher levels of occupational prestige. The full 2004 GSS survey did not include an extensive range of Internet use questions, but approximately one-third of the 2,812 respondents were randomly assigned an additional set of questions related to Internet use.

Comparing occupational prestige scores of individuals who use the Internet with those who do not results in a dramatic, statistically signif-icant difference.[3] On a prestige scale ranging from 17 to 86, the average occupational prestige score for Internet users was 48.3, compared with 37.3 for those who did not use the Internet. Table 4.2 presents more detailed information on the relationship between occupation type, occupational prestige, and Internet use. Here we see the six primary occupation types ranked by the percent of individuals in each category that uses the Internet. In the two highest categories, managerial and professional occupations, over 80 percent of respondents said they used the Internet. Among the two occupations with the lowest concentra-tion of Internet users—operators, fabricators and laborers, and farming, forestry, and fishing occupations—fewer than half of the respondents used the Internet.

Looking at the two rightmost columns of Table 4.2, the relationship between occupational prestige and Internet use is more complex within occupation types. The two occupational groups with levels of Internet use above 80 percent are also the groups with the highest average

Table 4.2 Occupation Type, Occupational Prestige, and Internet Use Among American Adults, 2004

| | PERCENT OF INTERNET USERS | AVERAGE OCCUPATION PRESTIGE RATING | |
		USE INTERNET	DO NOT USE INTERNET
Managerial/professional specialty occupations	87.4	59.4	57.1
Technical, sales, administrative support occupations	81.3	42.9	41.1
Service occupations	63.3	35.8**	29.6
Precision production, craft, repair occupations	53.5	43.8**	37.6
Operators, fabricators, and laborers	48.2	31.6	32.2
Farming, forestry, fishing occupations	26.3	35.0	29.1

Source: 2004 General Social Survey (GSS).
Note:
** $p < 0.01$. N = 831.

occupational prestige. Within these occupations, however, there is not a statistically significant difference in occupational prestige between individuals who use the Internet and those who do not. The two occupational groups with the lowest levels of Internet use also have lower average prestige scores. Yet within these occupations, too, there is no statistical difference in prestige between individuals who use the Internet and those who do not. In the two occupational groups in the middle, however, important differences emerge. Individuals in service occupations and precision production, craft, and repair occupations who do use the Internet have significantly *higher* average occupational prestige than those who do not.

Let's consider the effects of occupational prestige on Internet use relative to demographic and class variables. We'll use the same demographic variables that we did in Table 4.1, namely gender, race, and education. For class, we'll use family income.[4] Because we want to test whether class and status have independent effects on Internet use, we want to establish that family income, a proxy for class, and occupational prestige, a proxy for status, are independent of one another. The degree of correlation between family income and occupational prestige is represented by Figure 4.2, which plots data for the 831 respondents who provided family income and occupational prestige data; income is along the horizontal axis and prestige on the vertical axis. If family income and occupational prestige were positively and perfectly correlated with one another, the plotted points would fall in a line rising from left to right. Though there does appear to be some clustering of high prestige ratings at the high-income end of the scale, the correlation is far from perfect. A standard statistical measure of the degree of consistency between the two dimensions, which takes the square of the simple correlation between the two measures, would be one if these two dimensions were perfectly correlated and zero if they were completely independent of one another. In this case, the correlation coefficient equals 0.370 leading to a squared correlation of 0.137, which suggests a weak correlation at most.

Having established that family income and occupational prestige are relatively independent of one another, the next step is to determine the

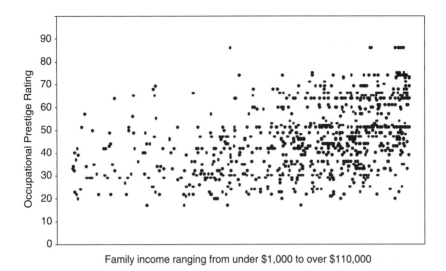

Figure 4.2 Family income and occupational prestige of American adults, 2004 (source: 2004 General Social Survey (GSS)). Pearson's correlation coefficient, r = 0.370. N = 831.

extent to which each is associated with Internet use. Model [1] in Table 4.3 uses the 2004 GSS data to replicate the key results reported in Model [2] of Table 4.1, which uses the Pew data. Relative to those with at least some college education, those with a high school degree or less were less likely to use the Internet. Similarly, individuals not working or retired were less likely to use the Internet than individuals who are working full or part-time. As was the case with the Pew study, GSS respondents with higher family incomes were more likely to use the Internet than those with lower family incomes. Model [2] in Table 4.3 adds occupational prestige to the equation. Here, we find that prestige, too, is positively and significantly related to Internet use. Although the impact of family income diminishes somewhat, its impact remains statistically significant. Assuming family income represents an individual's class situation, we can say that class and Internet use are related. Assuming occupational prestige represents social status, we can say that status and Internet use are also related. Note that neither income nor prestige "cause" an individual to use the Internet anymore than using the Internet "causes" higher income or greater occupational prestige.

Table 4.3 Effects of Education, Employment Status, Family Income, and Occupational Prestige on Odds of Using the Internet, 2004

	MODEL [1]	MODEL [2]
Less than high school degree: Some college or more	0.05**	0.09**
High school degree: Some college or more	0.27**	0.40**
Not employed: Employed full- or part-time	0.81	0.73**
Retired or disabled: Employed full- or part-time	0.64**	0.21**
Family income	1.10**	1.08**
Occupational prestige		1.04**
Nagelkerke Pseudo R2	0.368	0.390
Sample size	831	831

Source: 2004 General Social Survey (GSS).
Note:
** $p < 0.01$.

These measures are simply related. Nonetheless, they indicate that the link between the Internet and inequality is multi-dimensional and not simply a matter of class.

Recall that, in addition to occupational prestige, family background plays an important role in determining one's social status. The 2004 GSS respondents were queried about the educational, occupational, and socio-economic background of their parents. Figure 4.3 summarizes these data, comparing parental education of Internet users and non-users. Here we see significant results for both fathers' and mothers' years of schooling. The average father of an Internet user completed over 12 years of education, compared with just under eight-and-a-half years for the fathers of non-Internet users. For mothers, the average difference is smaller but still statistically significant, with a difference of just under two years of schooling between mothers of Internet users and mothers of non-users. Figure 4.4 presents similar findings for fathers' and mothers' occupational prestige and socio-economic status. In each case, the results are the same: the mothers and fathers of Internet users had significantly higher levels of occupational prestige and socio-economic status than the fathers and mothers of non-users.

Table 4.4 adds the effect of parental background to the analysis presented in Table 4.3, which considers the extent to which Internet

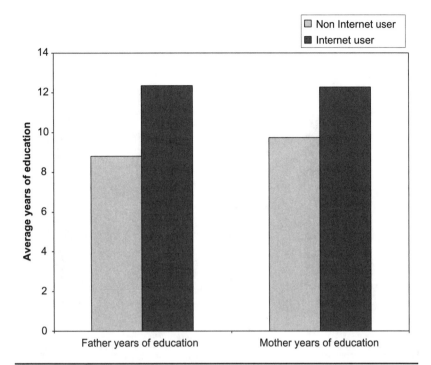

Figure 4.3 Internet use and parents' education, 2004 (source: 2004 General Social Survey (GSS)).

use varies with education, employment status, family income, and occupational prestige. In Model [1], there is a positive and significant effective of parental education on Internet use. Also in Model [1], education, family income, and occupational prestige remain positively and significantly correlated with Internet use, although the impact is weakened slightly once parental background is included in the analysis. In other words, individuals raised in a household with a higher level of parental education tend to obtain more education, live in families with higher incomes, and be employed in higher prestige occupations. These characteristics, in turn, are associated with increased odds of using the Internet. This analysis reveals that above and beyond these indirect effects, parental education has an independent, positive, and direct effect on Internet use as well.

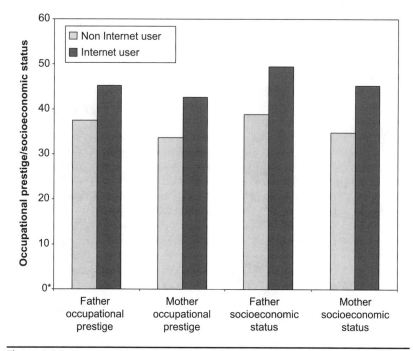

Figure 4.4 Internet use and parents' socio-economic status and occupational prestige, 2004
(source: 2004 General Social Survey (GSS)).
* NORC/GSS Occupational Prestige Scale.

It's possible that the effect of parents' education on Internet use is spurious, meaning that parental education has no effect at all, but appears to have an effect because parents' education is related to another variable that *does* have an effect on Internet use. That other variable might be age, which we've established as having a strong relationship to Internet use. In this case, the real explanation might be that some individuals are less likely to use the Internet because of their older age and not because their parents have lower levels of education.[5] To address this concern, Model [2] in Table 4.4 restricts the analysis to individuals under the age of 45. Model [2] also removes the control for retirement status since, by definition, individuals under the age of 45 are under the retirement age. Here, we see some weakening of the effects of the other variables, but not parental education, which actually gains strength and remains statistically significant. Occupational

Table 4.4 Effects of Education, Employment Status, Family Income, Occupational Prestige, and Parents' Education on Odds of Using the Internet, 2004

	ALL EMPLOYED ADULTS	EMPLOYED ADULTS UNDER 45
	MODEL [1]	MODEL [2]
Less than high school degree: Some college or more	0.11**	0.07**
High school degree: Some college or more	0.42**	0.28**
Not employed: Employed full- or part-time	0.62	0.65
Retired or disabled: Employed full- or part-time	0.27**	
Family income	1.06**	1.07**
Occupational prestige	1.03**	1.02
Parents' education	1.14**	1.17**
Nagelkerke Pseudo R2	0.378	0.307
Sample size	757	377

Source: 2004 General Social Survey (GSS).
Note:
** $p < 0.01$.

prestige is no longer statistically significant in Model [2], although this is probably due to the fact that by focusing on younger individuals, we've cut the sample in half.[6] Thus, family background, which we're using as a proxy for social status, has a strong and independent effect on Internet use. As the cultural perspective would predict, this effect is independent of, but related to, social class, which is also shown to have a strong effect.

Having established that there are independent class and status effects on Internet use, let's explore whether Internet use constitutes a kind of lifestyle. Specifically, we want to see whether Internet use occurs over multiple domains—information *and* communication, production *and* consumption. If it does, then we can say that high prestige individuals form a type of status group on account of their Internet lifestyle. As we saw in Chapter 1, which outlined a brief history of the Internet, online activities have developed from single isolated tools for specific purposes to collections of applications that heavy users integrate into the fabric of their daily lives. Today's well-off, well-educated consumer looking for a new dishwasher doesn't just go to a couple of stores and pick the best model he or she sees. Rather, he or she "Googles" a product type, compares several models by features and price, opens another browser tab and checks his or her available credit balance online, and orders the product online. Any number of similar scenarios could be described: researching a college for a child, coordinating an evening out with a significant other, searching for job opportunities in a new community. Thus, online activities leave different footprints on the lives of Americans and these footprints may vary with class position and social status.

To show these different footprints, we've superimposed a graph on the two axes of Internet use described in Chapter 2. The two axes of Internet use, again, are communication/information and production/ consumption (see Figure 2.14). Along with the four Internet activities characteristic of the end points of each continuum, we've added eight other Internet activities that fall within particular quadrants. For example, "writing a blog" is in the production/communication quadrant, while "reading a blog" is in the consumption/communication quadrant. There are 12 spokes on each graph and the area in the center of the graph is defined by the percentage of members of a given group who participate in each of the activities. Figure 4.5 contains the online activity footprints for each of the four levels of educational attainment we've been discussing. Here, several patterns emerge. Most obviously, the size of the footprint grows dramatically with each level of education. Those with less than a high school degree have a footprint that amounts to under 2 percent of the total area; whereas those with a bachelor's degree or higher have a footprint that is 22 percent of the total. Taken as a whole, the footprint size for those with the highest levels of education is 14 times larger than the footprint for those with the lowest level of education.

We can also consider the overall shape of each footprint in relation to one another and in relation to the four quadrants. Online activity among those without a high school degree is concentrated along the vertical axis, encompassing communication and information, but with little related to production and consumption. Thus the online activity of

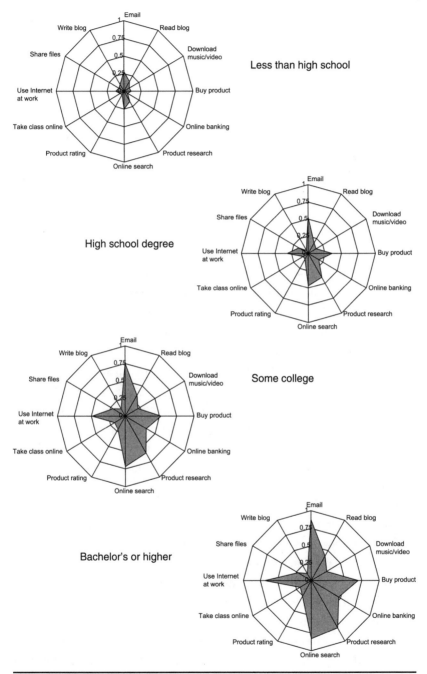

Figure 4.5 Online activity footprints by education, 2005 (source: Pew Internet & American Life, March 2005).

the less educated is primarily defined by email and online searches. With increasing levels of education, we see a growing percentage of individuals using the Internet for work and/or to buy products. Visually, the footprint takes on the shape of a four-pointed star. For those with some college education, and particularly those with a bachelor's degree or higher, a bulge appears in the star in the quadrant defined by information and consumption. This suggests that those with the highest levels of education are slightly more likely to get product information online than to actually purchase the product online. But as we saw in Chapter 2, the difference is not that great and nearly 70 percent of those with a bachelor's degree report that they have made purchases online.

Similar differences in size and shape of online activity footprints can be seen in Figure 4.6, where we consider family income. American adults in households with the highest incomes have footprints that are 24 percent of the total area, more than eight times larger than adults in households with incomes under $20,000. As was the case with education, higher income groups have a footprint that increasingly takes on the shape of a four-point star with a bulge in the quadrant defined by information and consumption. This bulge is somewhat more pronounced at the highest level of income than it was at the highest level of education. These results suggest that particular online lifestyles are associated with individuals in middle and upper classes. A cultural perspective would predict that these lifestyles would be related to status differences as well. Unfortunately, the GSS, which contains occupational measures, does not have the kind of Internet use information that would allow us to create online activity footprints for individuals in different occupations and at different levels of occupational prestige.[7] Because social prestige and social class are often correlated, we can infer that high-prestige individuals are likely to have larger online activity footprints of the kind we see here. In that respect, we may talk of a particular lifestyle associated with this status group.

Our initial consideration of the different online activity footprints suggests that different groups of Americans participate in Internet life to varying degrees and in different ways. But what exactly are

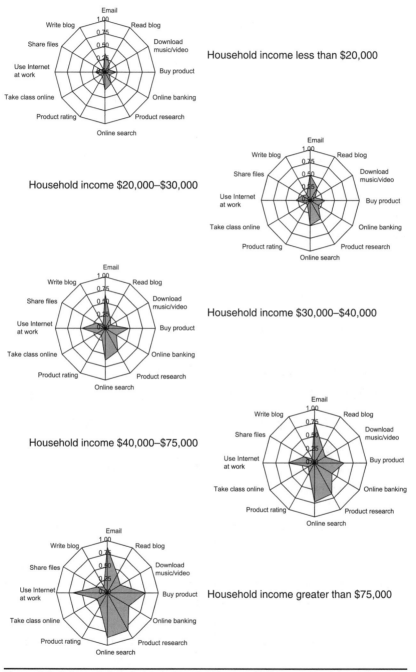

Figure 4.6 Online activity footprints by household income, 2005 (source: Pew Internet & American Life, March 2005).

individuals with smaller online footprints missing out on? And, why does it matter? In March 2005, the Pew Internet & American Life Project administered the "Major Moments Survey." This instrument asked respondents whether or not they had recently experienced a variety of important events. Some events were of a financial nature; others concerned issues of employment, health, and family. They followed up with those who had experienced different "major moments" to see what role the Internet had played in their decision-making regarding these events. Pew researchers John Horrigan and Lee Rainie (2006) found that the Internet was the most important source of information in these critical moments. They concluded that most individuals do not feel overwhelmed by the sheer quantity of online information and, indeed, find such information critical during major life events.

Our goal here is to reconsider these findings from a cultural perspective. We focus on the same set of major moments that were at the center of Horrigan and Rainie's work:

- Getting additional training for your career
- Helping another person with a major illness or medical condition
- Choosing a school or college for yourself or your child
- Buying a car
- Making a major investment or financial decision
- Finding a new place to live
- Changing jobs
- Dealing with a major illness or other health condition yourself

In addition to considering whether individuals were confronted with one of these events in the past two years, we consider how the use of the Internet at these times varied with educational level. We also determine if there are independent effects of income and education on participation in an Internet-oriented lifestyle. Then, we see if these class differences are still evident when we control for the influence of age, which we've already found to be an important correlate of online activity.

Table 4.5 Experience with Major Moments in the Past Two Years by Education, 2005

	ALL ADULTS (%)	< HIGH SCHOOL DEGREE (%)	HIGH SCHOOL DEGREE (%)	SOME COLLEGE (%)	BACHELOR'S OR HIGHER (%)
Getting additional training**	28.9	13.7	17.2	37.8	41.5
Helping another person with a major illness**	47.6	44.4	44.2	50.1	50.8
Choosing a school or college**	22.6	16.9	16.3	32.8	22.6
Buying a car	40.9	36.9	40.0	41.5	43.2
Making a major investment or financial decision**	34.9	19.0	26.3	39.0	49.4
Finding a new place to live	21.1	22.4	21.0	24.4	21.0
Changing jobs	21.1	18.5	20.6	22.1	22.1
Dealing with a major illness**	23.7	31.8	23.5	23.9	19.6

Source: Pew Internet & American Life, March 2005.
Note:
** $p < 0.01$.

As we can see in Table 4.5, dealing with five of these eight life moments varied with educational background: getting additional career training, helping another person with illness, choosing a school or college, making a major financial decision, and dealing with a medical condition. For example, in line with research suggesting that better educated individuals tend to be healthier, those with less than a high school degree were more than 50 percent more likely to have dealt with a major illness in the last two years compared with individuals with a bachelor's degree. In contrast, buying a car, finding a new place to live, and changing jobs were all "equal opportunity" moments in that roughly similar proportions of individuals reported experiencing these events across all levels of education. For a less educated segment of the population, then, online information related to education and health would be of tremendous help in major life moments. The question remains whether they actually had access to this information and/or knowledge of how to get access to this information.

Considering the extent to which individuals made use of the Internet in dealing with these major moments in Table 4.6, we see that individuals with a bachelor's degree were more than twice as likely to have used the Internet when buying a car or making a major financial decision than individuals with less than a high school degree. When it comes to finding a place to live, those with at least some college were over five times more likely to turn to the Internet to aid them in the process than those with less than a high school degree. Whether they were helping another person with a major illness or dealing with a major illness of their own, better educated individuals were significantly more likely to have turned to the variety of health information online. When it comes to changing jobs, we see that there was a difference in the use of the Internet according to education, but it was the least educated and the

Table 4.6 Use of the Internet in Major Moments in the Past Two Years by Education, 2005

DID YOU USE THE INTERNET TO GET INFORMATION WHEN DEALING WITH THE FOLLOWING . . .

	ALL ADULTS (%)	< HIGH SCHOOL DEGREE (%)	HIGH SCHOOL DEGREE (%)	SOME COLLEGE (%)	BACHELOR'S OR HIGHER (%)
Getting additional training	67.6	60.4	62.4	66.7	71.3
Helping another person with a major illness**	50.8	47.4	44.0	47.1	59.4
Choosing a school or college	65.4	72.9	67.5	60.8	69.1
Buying a car**	48.2	31.1	38.8	41.3	65.1
Making a major investment or financial decision**	53.5	30.8	36.2	51.8	64.7
Finding a new place to live**	48.5	11.6	31.5	57.5	58.3
Changing jobs**	40.5	44.6	35.2	33.9	49.6
Dealing with a major illness**	51.5	25.0	47.2	47.0	63.0

Source: Pew Internet & American Life, March 2005.
Note:
** $p < 0.01$.

most educated individuals who were more likely to have turned to the Internet. Those with a high school degree and those with some college education were less likely to have made use of the Internet for this purpose. The two areas where there is no relationship between level of education and use of the Internet are major moments related to education: getting additional career training and choosing a school or college for yourself or your child.

Figure 4.7 uses online footprints to summarize individuals' use of the Internet in major moments and how this varies with level of education. Looking across these graphs we see obvious differences in the size and shape of the footprints. The footprint for individuals with the lowest level of education occupies 17 percent of the total possible area; the footprint with individuals with the highest level of education occupies 39 percent of the total possible area. For those with the lowest level of education, we see an irregular shape to the footprint, which is produced by the relatively frequent use of the Internet for education-related major moments and the relatively infrequent use of the Internet for all other purposes.[8] Moving to higher levels of education, we see respondents reporting higher levels of use across the full range of major moments. Indeed, for those with at least a bachelor's degree, the footprint is nearly circular. With the exception of a job change, a relatively constant proportion of American adults with a bachelor's degree turned to the Internet when facing key decisions around a wide range of issues. Both the size (large) and shape (circular) of this footprint suggests that, for the most educated Americans, the Internet is part of a high status lifestyle. Thus, Horrigan and Rainie's conclusion that "the Internet is the most important source of information in these critical moments" is true primarily for the well-educated and the well-off.

The first column of Table 4.7 shows the results of a logistic regression of age, education, and family income on whether or not an individual used the Internet when confronted by one of the eight major moments. Age, education, and family income all have statistically significant independent effects. Regardless of age or family income, individuals with a bachelor's degree were more likely to have gone online at these times than those with lower levels of education.

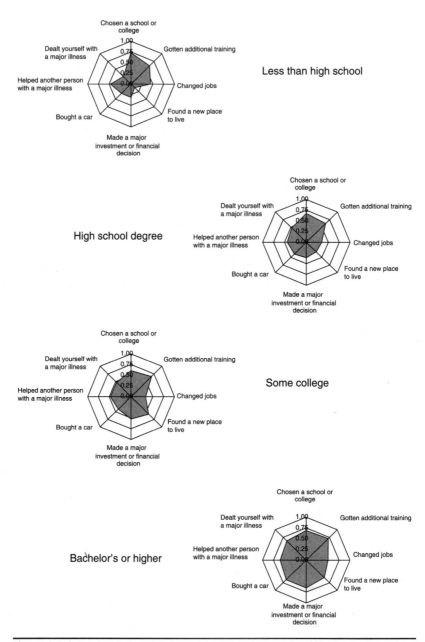

Figure 4.7 Online activity footprints for major moments by education, 2005 (source: Pew Internet & American Life, March 2005).

Regardless of age or education, individuals in households with incomes of $75,000 or more were more likely to have gone online at these times than those in households with lower incomes. And regardless of education and family income, younger adults were more likely to have gone online at these times than older adults. We see a similar pattern when we consider if an individual sends or reads email (column 2), if they do any work online for their job other than email (column 3), and if they research products online (column 4). Online activity for a variety of purposes, then, reflects differences in income and education. Class differences, then, are related to a package of online activities that suggest an Internet-intensive lifestyle.

The numbers reported in Table 4.7 are odds ratios indicating how a one-unit change in the independent variable affects the odds of one outcome rather than the other.[9] Looking at column 1 of Table 4.7, we

Table 4.7 Effects of Age, Education, and Family Income on Odds of Using Internet for Selected Purposes, 2005

ESTIMATED ODDS RATIO FOR GOING ONLINE TO . . .			
	DEAL WITH MAJOR MOMENT [1]	SEND OR READ EMAIL [2]	WORK OTHER THAN EMAIL [3]	RESEARCH PRODUCTS [4]
Age	0.960**	0.961**	0.967**	0.963**
Educational Achievement				
Less than high school degree	0.100**	0.064**	0.065**	0.076**
High school graduate	0.213**	0.170**	0.194**	0.236**
Some college	0.495**	0.447**	0.387**	0.539**
Bachelor's degree or higher	reference group			
Household Income				
Less than $20,000	0.221**	0.122**	0.128**	0.127**
$20,000 to under $30,000	0.418**	0.299**	0.299**	0.262**
$30,000 to under $40,000	0.393**	0.311**	0.298**	0.279**
$40,000 to under $75,000	0.709*	0.548**	0.588**	0.510**
$75,000 or more	reference group			
Proportion of variance explained	0.346	0.419	0.358	0.388
Sample size	1,909	2,201	2,201	2,200

Notes:
* $p < 0.05$;   ** $p < 0.01$.

see that age, regardless of educational level or family income, decreases the odds of using the Internet in a major moment. For each additional year of age, an individual is 4 percent less likely to use the Internet. In terms of education, individuals with less than a high school degree, regardless of age or family income, were 90 percent less likely to have used the Internet for a major moment than an individual with a bachelor's degree.[10] Looking at family income, those individuals with family incomes of less than $20,000 were 78 percent less likely to have used the Internet during major life events than individuals with household incomes of $75,000 and above. For all four Internet activities, age, education, and family income are each strongly and independently associated with use of the Internet.

Nowhere is an Internet lifestyle more evident than in Web2.0 applications, in which Internet use is so seamless and interactive that it constitutes a genuine social world. Surveys conducted in March of 2007 by the Pew Internet & American Life Project included an in-depth section on online video activities, which have become a hallmark of Web2.0. Viewing online video was unheard of in the early years of the Internet's popularity. YouTube, for example, did not launch until 2005. But by 2007, an estimated 57 percent of American adult Internet users had viewed videos online. Figure 4.8, however, indicates that among adults with low levels of education, online video viewing of any type is still relatively rare.[11] In contrast, for individuals with a bachelor's degree or higher, online video viewing is becoming a part of their daily lives. Close to half of all adults with a college degree had watched a news video online and more than one in four had watched a humor or comedy video.

As a Web2.0 activity, online video viewing is more than the simple act of watching a video; it involves collective sharing and social commentary. As Table 4.8 indicates, one-third of all adults with a bachelor's degree had sent a video link to someone else and nearly half had been sent such a link. By contrast, only about one in ten Americans with a high school degree or less had ever participated in online video sharing. As Table 4.9 suggests, the social aspect of online video viewing extends beyond the one-to-one sharing of links to include the

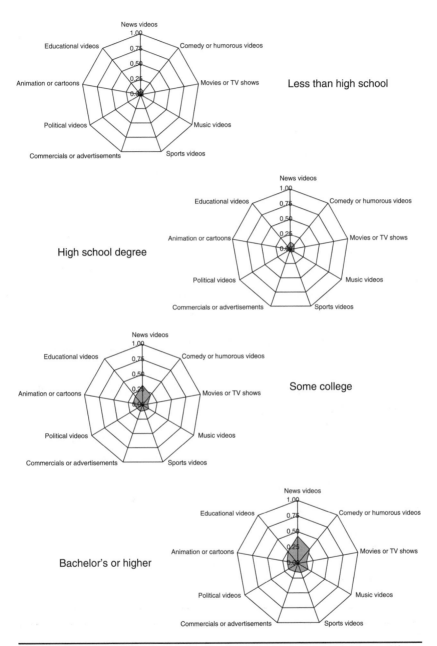

Figure 4.8 Viewing of online video by education, 2007 (source: Pew Internet & American Life, February 2007).

Table 4.8 One-to-One Sharing of Online Video by Education, 2007

HOW OFTEN, IF EVER . . .	ALL ADULTS (%)	< HIGH SCHOOL DEGREE (%)	HIGH SCHOOL DEGREE (%)	SOME COLLEGE (%)	BACHELOR'S OR HIGHER (%)
. . . HAVE YOU SENT SOMEONE ELSE A LINK TO A VIDEO?[1]					
at least a few times a month	9.0	3.5	4.6	10.2	15.5
less often	10.8	3.0	5.3	14.6	17.8
never	80.2	93.5	90.2	75.2	66.7
. . . DOES SOMEONE ELSE SEND YOU A LINK TO A VIDEO?[2]					
at least a few times a month	18.6	5.5	9.0	23.6	31.6
less often	9.5	2.8	4.4	12.6	16.2
never	71.9	91.7	86.5	63.8	52.2

Source: Pew Internet & American Life Project, February 2007 data collection.
Notes:
1 N = 2006, χ^2 = 144.83 with 6 degrees of freedom, $p < 0.001$.
2 N = 2002, χ^2 = 239.45 with 6 degrees of freedom, $p < 0.001$.

Table 4.9 One-to-Many Sharing of Online Video by Education, 2007

HOW OFTEN, IF EVER . . .	ALL ADULTS (%)	< HIGH SCHOOL DEGREE (%)	HIGH SCHOOL DEGREE (%)	SOME COLLEGE (%)	BACHELOR'S OR HIGHER (%)
. . . have you shared a link to a video by posting it on a website or blog?[1]	2.4	0.9	0.5	2.3	5.2
. . . have you rated a video you saw on the Internet using a rating system?[2]	3.4	3.2	1.3	4.3	5.4
. . . have you posted a comment after you saw a video online?[3]	3.0	2.5	1.2	3.2	5.2
. . . have you uploaded a video file online where others can watch it?[4]	4.5	0.9	2.5	5.5	7.8

Source: Pew Internet & American Life Project, February 2007 data collection.
Notes:
1 N = 2006, χ^2 = 32.71 with 3 degrees of freedom, $p < 0.001$.
2 N = 2007, χ^2 = 12.86 with 3 degrees of freedom, $p < 0.005$.
3 N = 2006, χ^2 = 19.81 with 3 degrees of freedom, $p < 0.001$.
4 N = 2004, χ^2 = 27.19 with 3 degrees of freedom, $p < 0.001$.

one-to-many sharing of content that is characteristic of Web2.0. Online videos are rated, commented on, and linked by personal blogs and profiles, with individuals putting up their own videos for collective and anonymous review. At the time of the Pew survey in March 2007, these were activities in which only a small percentage of American adults participated. And it appears that that small percent was constituted by the well-educated. In sum, Web2.0 is certainly not a lifestyle of the "rich and famous," but it *is* a lifestyle of the well-off and well-educated.

Summary and Conclusion

In Chapter 2, we reviewed the extent to which the Internet and a number of online activities have become central to the lives of millions of Americans. As we demonstrated, however, participation in a variety of online activities is not uniformly distributed throughout the population of Internet users and even less so among the entire U.S. adult population. Depending on the activity in question, variation was found according to a number of key demographic and socio-economic characteristics. The most consistent and striking sources of variation were found along the traditional markers of class, namely education and income. These markers were important to Max Weber, who emphasized how members of distinct social classes had different life chances. For Weber, however, inequality was multi-dimensional and included not simply class, but status as well. Drawing heavily from the sociology of Weber, we considered a more culturally oriented theory of social inequality and its relevance for differences in Internet use. Specifically, we demonstrated how occupational prestige and family background channel individuals into differential lifestyles, which in turn mark, culturally, enduring social divides. One of those cultural markers is Internet use.

The empirical analyses in this chapter used these theoretical insights to evaluate the relative effects of status and class on Internet use and Internet activities. These analyses revealed that education and income independently affected the odds that an individual used the Internet on the previous day. They also demonstrated that Internet use varied with occupations and occupational prestige, two common sources of status in Western society. Considering family background, another source of social prestige, we found that parental background influenced Internet use above and beyond the effects of education, income, and occupational prestige. To understand the significance of these differences, we considered online activity footprints for different segments of American society. Better-off and better-educated Americans left online footprints many times larger than the poorest and least-educated segments of American society. Moreover, the online footprints for more privileged members of American society were more extensive, indicating online activities associated with consumption and production, as well as information and communication. The intensive and extensive nature of Internet use among the well-off and well-educated suggests an elite lifestyle from which the poor and uneducated are marginalized. This lifestyle extends into major life moments. Although we did not have data to test whether this lifestyle was associated with particular differences in status, we inferred some association given the degree to which education, income, and prestige are correlated.

Comparing the cultural approach with the conflict approach, we can see that each lends a unique perspective on the relationship between the Internet and inequality. The conflict perspective emphasizes how Internet skills are used by middle-class Americans to leverage labor markets and pass class advantage on to children. The cultural perspective draws attention to how particular Internet activities define an elite lifestyle. Both perspectives add something to our analysis of the "digital divide." That is, we may interpret these approaches as being complementary rather than competing explanations for Internet inequality. In the next chapter, we'll tackle a third perspective, which highlights the role that these inequalities play in upholding a larger social system. Specifically, we'll look at the functionalist perspective, which approaches inequality in a rather different way from the conflict and cultural approaches.

Questions for Reading, Reflection, and Debate

1 At the beginning of this chapter, we used the example of Facebook to illustrate how status groups are formed on the Internet and how rules of social interaction exclude lower status individuals from membership in high status groups. Using this example of Facebook, can you think of ways in which class, as opposed to status, determines who becomes "friends"? Are there instances on Facebook in which members of two different social classes might find themselves "friends" (i.e., part of the same status group)? In thinking through these questions, consider your own social networks and how they are limited to individuals who are like you in terms of status and class and/or how they are open to individuals who are unlike you in these respects.

2 We have suggested throughout this chapter that Internet use constitutes a kind of middle-class lifestyle from which the poor and uneducated are excluded. Given how prevalent Internet use is in the general U.S. population, this argument may be hard to sell. Is Internet use, even extensive and intensive Internet use, akin to gourmet restaurants, designer clothes, and Ivy League colleges—a cultural means through which wealthy individuals define their status? Using examples from the web, present evidence for and against this cultural perspective. In particular, think through examples like online dating (e.g., e-Harmony), online news sources (e.g., Huffington Post), and online commerce (e.g., eBay).

3 Most often, we consider elite social classes and high status groups when thinking about how Internet use and social class/status are related. Consider, instead, how less educated, poorer, and less prestigious individuals use the Internet. Which websites do you think they are likely to frequent? And how do these online activities constitute a kind of lower class e-culture? How might these websites or online activities define or reinforce a working-class identity or working-class culture—both on- and offline?

4 A central theme in this chapter is that what we do online signifies what class we belong to and in what status group we enjoy membership. Other than limiting ourselves to particular online activities and particular online groups, how might we "mark" ourselves as belonging to different social classes and status groups when we are engaged in the same activities online? Is it possible that even when different social classes and status groups are online, and even when they are engaged in the same activities, they might still be marking themselves culturally in different ways? How might you analyze user profiles on Match.com, the popular online dating service, to answer these questions?

5 In tackling the relationship between status and Internet use, we run quickly into a chicken-or-egg dilemma. It could be that high status individuals participate in certain Internet activities, marking these activities as "cool" and according them high prestige as a result. Or, it could be that certain Internet activities are "cool," attracting high-status individuals to them. In terms of the "coolness" or "it" factor, which comes first? The status group or the technological innovation? In exploring this question, consider the rise and popularity of YouTube.

5

INTERNET INEQUALITY FROM A FUNCTIONALIST PERSPECTIVE

As we advance in the evolutionary scale, the ties which bind the individual to his family, to his native soil, to traditions which his past has given him, to collective group usages, become loose. . . . This is what gives moral value to the division of labor. Through it, the individual becomes cognizant of his dependence upon society; from it come the forces which keep him in check and restrain him.
—*Durkheim* 1933, pp. 400–1

In his analysis of how societies manage disease outbreaks, Johnson (2006) argues that new information technologies have the potential to connect grassroots information and professional expertise. As he argues: "It has never been easier for . . . local knowledge to find its way onto a map, making patterns of health and sickness (as well as less perilous matters) visible to experts and laypeople in new ways" (Johnson 2006, pp. 218–19). In Johnson's formulation, the public benefits from information technology whether or not all members of society are online. Internet inequalities notwithstanding, everyone benefits from the management of disease outbreaks using Internet technology. This is a provocative argument that flies in the face of public concern over the "digital divide." Does it matter that many individuals do not use the Internet on a daily basis if, in the end, society benefits from information and innovations provided by the Internet? This question gets to the heart of the functionalist perspective. From a functionalist viewpoint, what matters most is not whether everyone is online, but whether society benefits in some way from Internet technology.

A strong emphasis on the functional role played by social institutions like the Internet distinguishes the functionalist perspective from the conflict and cultural perspectives. Emile Durkheim, an important early functionalist theorist, speaks of this cohesive role in the opening quote above. According to Durkheim, each society has a particular division of labor that requires individuals to play a specialized role in society. This division of labor provides great returns for society and for individuals, since societies benefit from tasks accomplished by each individual and since individuals specialize in those tasks for which they are most suited. Social institutions (e.g., the school system, the family, etc.) provide the structural framework that connects individuals to their respective roles. Thus, families channel children to undertake certain tasks in society. For some individuals, this might mean having children and being a stay-at-home parent; for others, this might mean becoming president of the United States. In either case, individuals are channeled into roles in which they display some talent. And in fulfilling those roles, they help keep society running smoothly. According to Durkheim, this overarching institutional framework, the division of labor that it facilitates, and the roles that it upholds constitute society. During most historical moments, that society is relatively stable and orderly. Everyone plays some part; everyone depends on one another; and everyone is committed to the larger collective.

According to Durkheim, inequality is fundamental to this division of labor. That is, some people are rewarded more than others for the roles that they play in society. And the reason for this is that there must be some incentive or reward system to encourage people to take on the really important, or most functional, roles in society. Because the division of labor functions to integrate society and instill social order, inequality is justified. In a sense, the ends (social order and cohesion) justify the means (social inequality). In this chapter we will explore the functionalist perspective on inequality, starting with the classic work of Durkheim. After considering the theoretical implications of this approach for the relationship between the Internet and inequality, we'll consider empirical evidence related to this relationship. In keeping with the functionalist emphasis on social structure, the evidence in this chapter primarily draws on Internet content, or the text and links found on web pages that represent a kind of online social structure. In particular, we'll look at the website Yahoo! and the extent to which it caters to a privileged subset of users, even while providing benefits to a larger community.

Social Structure and Internet Use

Throughout much of his life, Durkheim was intrigued by how modern societies held together unique and autonomous individuals. He wanted to know how societies compelled their members to work together as a group for collective survival and prosperity. With few exceptions, he argued, most individuals depend on one another to survive. But this interdependency produces tension between individual autonomy and freedom, on the one hand, and group obligations and responsibility, on the other. Durkheim posited that, in most cases and during most historical moments, social laws and norms encourage individuals to act in the interest of the group. In his classic work, *The Division of Labor in Society*, Durkheim laid out this argument, explaining that social norms and consensus compel members of society to act for the good of society as a whole.

One of the reasons that individuals tend to work together is that they feel a sense of solidarity with others in their society. In *The Division of Labor in Society*, Durkheim distinguishes between different types of solidarity. "Mechanical solidarity" is characteristic of earlier societies, in which the division of labor is limited. In these societies, individuals carry out more or less the same tasks. Shared work constitutes a form of "collective consciousness," which bonds individuals together. "Organic solidarity," in contrast, is characteristic of modern societies, in which the division of labor is extensive. In these societies, individuals carry out highly specialized tasks. A commonly cited example here is occupational specialization. As societies become more complex, some individuals take on the role of healer, others the role of teacher and leader. Over time, occupations develop around these roles and we have doctors, professors, and politicians. Eventually, we have even greater specialization, with some doctors specializing in pediatrics, some professors specializing in molecular biology, and some politicians specializing in local city councils. This specialization is a means to facilitate productive coexistence rather than destructive competition (Durkheim 1933, p. 267). Indeed, specialization creates a new form of interdependency and a new basis for solidarity. It is this form of "organic solidarity" that is of major concern to Durkheim—and to us—since it characterizes social life in modern societies.

According to Durkheim and other functionalists, each role or task that is fulfilled by an individual in society is differentially rewarded. Some individuals are rewarded through higher salaries, others through greater prestige. In most cases, these rewards are based on merit; they provide an incentive for individuals to invest in the training and time to take on particular roles in the division of labor. Although efficient in terms of producing an effective division of labor, this reward system produces some level of inequality. That is, some individuals are rewarded more than others on account of their talents and training. In this sense, "an ever growing inequality" is a fundamental feature of the modern division of labor (Durkheim 1933, p. 379). Durkheim considered such inequality legitimate—a small price to pay for the social order and collective good it ensured. Without inequality, we would have no division of labor; and without the division of labor, we would have no social order, no society. To some, this issue has been grounds to treat Durkheim as an apologist for the existing social order and see functionalism as a conservative justification for inequality as a means to maintain the status quo. A careful reading of Durkheim, however, reveals that he clearly distinguishes between legitimate forms of inequality (i.e., those based on merit) from illegitimate forms of inequality (i.e., those based on gender, race or family background). The latter, in Durkheim's view, are illegitimate in that they give "advantages to some which are not necessarily in keeping with their personal worth" (Durkheim 1933, p. 378).

Since Durkheim's formulation, scholars have refined and expanded on the functionalist perspective. In "An Analytical Approach to the Theory of Social Stratification" (1940), for example, the American sociologist Talcott Parsons examines how social stratification reflects social stability and consensus. In particular, he demonstrates how "the differential ranking of human individuals" in society is based on socially agreed upon ideas of the relative importance of certain societal roles versus others. Likewise, in "Some Principles of Stratification" (1945), Kinsley Davis and Wilbert Moore explore "the requirement faced by any society of placing and motivating individuals in the social structure" (Davis and Moore 1945, p. 217). To induce individuals to fill certain jobs and perform certain tasks, particularly those that are disagreeable or require a great deal of training, societies must attach different rewards to different positions. Positions that are of the greatest importance for society (i.e., the most functional) are ranked highest. For example, if we do not reward medical doctors with high salaries and prestige, how would we ensure that talented individuals invest in years of expensive medical training to become doctors? Although this incentive system means that some individuals will be paid more than others, it also means that society as a whole will benefit from the medical services of well-trained doctors.

Functionalism's critics are too numerous to summarize individually (Tumin 1953; Buckley 1958, 1963; Wesolowski 1962; Huaco 1963; Stinchcombe 1963; Broom and Cushing 1977); it is sufficient to note the main bases of criticism. First, a number of critics point to the ambiguous character of "functional importance." According to the functionalist perspective, some roles are more functionally important than others, and they should be rewarded as such. Members of society generally agree on which roles these are, leading to consensus on the distribution of rewards in society. Yet it's easy to think of positions in society that are "functionally important," but not well-paid or regarded. Just as easily, we can think of highly compensated and regarded positions that are less functionally important. According to the U.S. Bureau of Labor Statistics, for example, there will be a growing demand for both event planners and childcare workers in the next 20 years. The median salary for the former is currently $42,180; the median salary for the latter is currently $17,630. Is the social value or functional importance of an event planner really more than double that of a childcare worker? Nearly all critics also question the consensual orientation of functionalist theory. Ranking and rewards are most likely defined by those in power, rather than by consensus of all individuals in society. Power also helps influence the rank attained, with many high-ranking individuals achieving their rank not by talent alone, but with family connections and resources as well.

Another important criticism landing at the feet of functionalism is what social theorists refer to as "social determinism." In attending to the role of social forces in directing human action, functionalism has the tendency to obscure the role played by individuals in society; individuals become mere puppets whose actions are directed from above. This kind of social determinism is nowhere more evident than in the work of Durkheim, who emphasized the relative importance of social structure and its coercive effects on human action. According to Durkheim, there were social facts, or social forces, that existed outside the individual and served to guide and even limit individual behavior:

> Not only are these types of behaviour and thinking external to the individual, but they are endued with a compelling and coercive power by virtue of which, whether he wishes it or not, they impose themselves upon him. Undoubtedly when I conform to them of my own free will, this coercion is not felt or felt hardly at all, since it is unnecessary. None the less it is intrinsically a characteristic of these facts; the proof of this is that it asserts itself as soon as I try to resist. (Durkheim [1895] 1938, p. 50)

Through the division of labor, the individual becomes cognizant of his or her dependence upon society, an awareness that restrains him or her from pursuing their own interests (Durkheim 1933, p. 43). Durkheim did not understand social structure as something that was imposed by some nameless, faceless social coordinator from above. Rather, it emerged through the self-coordinated actions of individuals.

In this respect, contemporary functionalists refer to Durkheim as an "emergence" theorist (Poggi 2000; Sawyer 2002). The V-shape formation of a flock of birds, for example, is not created or maintained in top down fashion; rather, it *emerges* as individual pairs of birds coordinate their flight paths with one another (Sawyer 2002, p. 229). Though Durkheim appreciated the role of the individual in creating social structure, he is seen as a theorist that did not quite grasp the delicate interplay between individual action and social forces. Thus, contemporary functionalists argue that attention needs to be concentrated somewhere between the individual and society (Sawyer 2002). This line of study has been followed especially in the Sociology of Culture, where patterns of behavior and taste are considered to be shaped and maintained by social networks (DiMaggio 1987; Erickson 1996; Mark 2003). Here and elsewhere, social networks are seen as a site wherein human action and social forces intersect in more complex ways than Durkheim outlined.

These criticisms notwithstanding, functionalism provides multiple angles through which to explore Internet technology and its role in society. The idea of a division of labor in which some are rewarded for their functional skills and contributions, for example, lends itself to one interpretation of the Internet, in which those with Internet skills are rewarded with higher earnings. Frank Levy and Richard Murnane, in their book *The New Division of Labor: How Computers are Creating the Next Job Market* (2004), argue that computing technology has affected "the distribution of jobs in the economy and the skills those jobs demand" (p. 30). There are jobs, they note, that neither computers nor many people are capable of performing, such as jobs that require analysis of complex patterns using computer technology. Individuals who can perform such work are well-remunerated because they can do the work that computers cannot and because they invest in the training and education necessary to perform these tasks.

Rather than test the claims made by Levy and Murnane, we're going to do a different kind of analysis in this chapter. Given the attention to social structure by the functionalist perspective, we'll focus on the structure of the Internet to explore the relationship between the individual

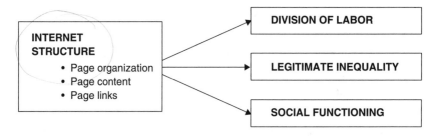

Figure 5.1 Model for the functionalist perspective.

and the larger society. The Internet provides a unique window into social functioning in that it can stand in for society as a whole. From a Durkheimian perspective, individual actions should be channeled or directed by the structure of the Internet. As well, individual users should be differentially rewarded by this Internet structure. That is, we should see some manifestation of inequality in rewards associated with Internet use. Most importantly, this Internet structure should produce some larger social good, or provide some social function to justify this unequal reward system. Figure 5.1 illustrates the theoretical model from a functionalist perspective, depicting the influence of Internet structure on individual action, social inequality, and social functioning.

Internet Organization as Social Structure

During the years when the Pew data were collected, public portals (e.g., Yahoo! and AOL) were the typical Internet user's entryway into the Internet. These portals included, and continue to include, what we call "content channels." Content channels are things like news headlines, health and diet tips, and entertainment information, which are designed to keep users at the portal and focused on the portal's online advertising for as long as possible. Given this structure and purpose, portals are an excellent window into Internet structure. Yahoo! has long been the leading public portal and was still the most visited website as of May 2008.[1] Therefore, we'll focus on Yahoo! to explore the functionalist perspective, especially its claims that social structure coordinates individual action to produce a division of labor.

As described in the popular press, Yahoo!'s origins are the stuff of dot.com legend. Begun in 1994 by David Filo and Jerry Yang, two graduate students in electrical engineering at Stanford University, Yahoo! was initially intended to help its founders keep track of places they found of interest on the Internet. Very much in the spirit of the early Internet, the name Yahoo! was selected for its self-deprecating connotation,[2] not to mention that it served equally well as a self-effacing acronym: "Yet Another Hierarchical Officious Oracle." Word-of-mouth quickly attracted a user base and, by the fall of 1994, Yahoo! experienced its first million-hit-day with over 100,000 unique visitors. Venture capital funding of two million dollars came in 1995 and was followed by a very successful initial public offering (IPO) in April of 1996. Since then Yahoo! growth has been nothing short of phenomenal. At the time of the initial IPO, there were 49 Yahoo! employees; by 2007, there were 12,000 Yahoo! employees at 25 facilities around the world.

Looking at an early Yahoo! home page from May 16, 1996 (Figure 5.2), the portal is easily recognizable. Organized around 14 categories, Yahoo! was little more than a listing of recommended sites. Following Filo and Yang's original model, these categories were populated with links selected by Yahoo! employees. By the fall of 1996, the site was encouraging visitors to recommend sites of interest as well. Later efforts to focus on "cool sites," "Buzz," and "What Yahoos are looking for" attempted to more fully exploit the collective intelligence of its user community. That is, users were invited to share their own links to build up the Yahoo! directory, creating an ever larger web of Internet links for others to enjoy.

By way of contrast, Figure 5.3 presents a more recent Yahoo! home page, this one from October 17, 2006. The look and feel of this page are quite different. As you'll see, the directory section is downsized from 14 to 12 categories, with no subcategories. As well, it is positioned toward the bottom of the page. By the end of 2007, the directory section would be gone altogether, while "Pulse: What Yahoos Are Into" and "Top Search" sections would be featured. Compared with 1996, however, the biggest changes in Yahoo! were the level of complexity and the extent to which the site was redefined as a portal for commercial activity. The

Figure 5.2 Yahoo! home page from October 17, 1996 (source: reproduced with permission of Yahoo! Inc. © 2009 Yahoo! Inc. YAHOO! and the YAHOO! logo are registered trademarks of Yahoo! Inc.).

site's complexity is visually evident. The commercial orientation is apparent through close inspection. Directly below the Yahoo! logo is a link to obtain a free credit report. Finance, real estate, shopping, the yellow pages, business, auctions, and classified are all separate links. Yahoo! Small Business, Marketplace, and Yahoo! Advertising Solutions are separate rubrics with multiple links tied to economic activity. In this particular web page, even the Yahoo! Tech section is about promoting sales of camcorders in order to "Save Summer Memories."

Although the comparison of these two Yahoo! home pages suggests that Internet content has become increasingly complex and commercialized, a more rigorous, systematic analysis is needed to confirm this

Figure 5.3 Yahoo! home page from May 17, 2006 (source: reproduced with permission of Yahoo! Inc. © 2009 Yahoo! Inc. YAHOO! and the YAHOO! logo are registered trademarks of Yahoo! Inc.).

impression. For this, ten randomly selected Yahoo! home pages were downloaded for each year between 1996 and 2005, providing a sample of 100 pages to analyze for changes in Yahoo! over time. For each page, we tracked the number of words to quantify page complexity. As the dotted line in Figure 5.4 indicates, the number of words increased nearly four-fold in this time frame, from over 100 words in 1996 to just over 400 in 2005. An interesting anomaly to the pattern of gradual

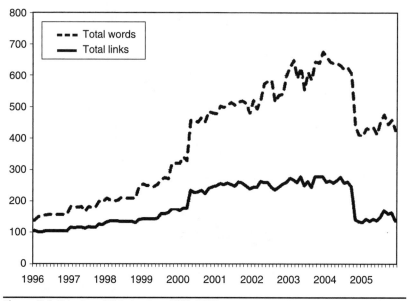

Figure 5.4 Yahoo! word link structure, 1996–2005.

growth can be seen between June of 2000 and November of 2004. This period began with a spike of an additional 200 words, followed by a return of gradual growth, a loss of approximately 200 words in 2004, and a return to the pattern of gradual growth. The solid line in Figure 5.4 represents the number of links found on each page. Here, too, three distinct phases are apparent. Through the first half of 2000, there is a gradual increase in the number of links on the page, followed by a noticeable spike in June of 2000. Between 2000 and 2004, the number of links levels off before falling. By the end of the observation period, the number of links on the Yahoo! home page is essentially the same as in 1996. The average number of words, however, has increased nearly three-fold.

The sharp increase in words and links in 2000 was chiefly due to the addition of a number of links to other Yahoo! informational pages, clustered together at the bottom of the page under "More Yahoo!s" These links often used the keywords (e.g., Finance or Movies) that were found on the top of the page in the major information categories that were the building blocks of the Yahoo! home page back in 1996. In the summer of 2002, there are two further changes in the organization of information on the Yahoo! home page. First, the basic information categories were no longer listed alphabetically. Importantly, the category "Arts & Humanities" is moved down to the second half of the list and "Business & Economy" is moved to the top of the list. Second, the categories under "More Yahoo!s" are reduced in number. Specifically, headings such as "Entertainment," "News," and "Publishing" are eliminated, leaving just four categories: "Guides," "Small Business," "Enterprise," and "Personal Finance." After the fall of 2004, the basic informational categories are nowhere to be seen. The left-hand side of the page is topped by a list of relatively narrow topics organized alphabetically from "Autos" to the "Yellow Pages." These links are then followed by a block reserved for a featured product advertisement. The remainder of the left-hand side is broken into categories including: "Yahoo! Featured," "Small Business," "Entertainment," "Buzz log—What the world is searching for…," "Yahoo! Web Directory," and "More Yahoo! Services." The right-hand side is divided into three main sections: "In the News," "Weather and Traffic," and "Marketplace."

These changes are more than matters of editorial decision-making and efforts to improve the user experience. The content and organization of these categories, which determine the links that users may follow from a portal's home page, guide the user down particular content streams.[3] A detailed examination of the links making up the Yahoo! home pages during this time period reveals that these streams of information are not random or haphazard, but are deliberate and intentional. In particular, the shift in design and content reflects an increasingly commercialized Internet portal that caters to a particular user audience. To better assess the shifting content of the Yahoo! home page, each of the 18,847 links on the sample pages were coded. Initial codes were based on the categories of online activities used in the Pew survey (e.g., product research, sending email, looking for employment).

Coding links using activity categories does not necessarily imply that individuals clicking on these links undertook those activities. For example, clicking on a link such as "Yahoo! Shopping—Digital

Cameras" could be for the purpose of buying a camera or researching cameras.[4] In the coding of links for this chapter, each link was assigned only one category, with the context of the page determining the code assigned. In Figure 5.3, for example, the box "In the News" features links to NBA, NHL, and so on. These links could be interpreted as obtaining sports information. In this case, however, we coded based on context, which suggested that these links were related to obtaining news. A second round of coding, allowing for multiple codes per link, will be needed to determine how sensitive the findings are to coding ambiguities. For now, these issues are mitigated through aggregation. That is, similar activities are grouped together to create broad, umbrella-like activity categories. For example, the code "Consumption" in Table 5.1 includes links identified as product research, as well as those links identified as product purchase. Thus, the outcome is the same regardless of which code was selected.

Table 5.1 provides an overview of the distribution of links according to these categories across the entire time period. Between 1996 and 2005, information related to a hobby/interest or to a particular geographical area accounts for one-third of all links on Yahoo! home pages. Consumption activities represent just over 10 percent of all links. What we're really interested in, however, is how links have changed over time on Yahoo!'s home page. Table 5.2 breaks the categorization of links into the three phases identified in Figure 5.3. Here, we see a clear redefinition of Yahoo! away from its origins as a directory of recommended links. Twenty six percent of links during the period from 1996 through June of 2000 (Phase I) fall into the category of "information on a hobby or interest." By the end of the observation period, from November 2004 through December 2005 (Phase III), only 11 percent of the links fell into this category. An even larger rate of decline was found in the percentage of links that provided information about specific geographic areas; more than 18 percent of the links were of this type in Phase I, a percentage that declined to 6 percent in Phase III. A significant decline is also apparent in the percentage of links related to health; they were half as common in Phase III (2 percent) as in Phase I (4 percent). In contrast, the number of links tied to consumption

Table 5.1 Classification of Links on Yahoo! Home Page, 1996–2005

	PERCENT
Information related to a hobby or interest	18.7
Information related to a specific geographic area	15.1
Consumption—product research, travel, purchase products, real estate	10.2
Entertainment—movies, music, TV, and sports	8.2
Yahoo! site-related information	7.5
News	5.7
Communication—email, IM, chat, dating sites, online groups	4.8
Production—looking for a job or any work-related activity except email	4.8
Health—general health, specific diseases or fitness	3.0
Financial information	3.0
Use of a search engine	2.4
Other*	16.7
Total (N = 18,847)	100.0

Percentages may not equal 100% due to rounding.

Note:

* Other types include: check weather reports and forecasts, get news or information about politics and the campaign, just for fun or to pass the time, bank online, play a lottery or gamble online, play online games, look for religious or spiritual information online, download music files, take a class online for credit toward a degree, search for a map or driving directions, use the internet to get photos developed or display, make a donation to a charity online, create a web log or "blog," use online classified ads or sites like Craigslist. None of the activities in this category include more than 3% of the links.

nearly doubled, from 8 percent in Phase I to 13 percent in Phase III. The "Entertainment" category experienced a similar level of growth, from 6 percent in Phase I to 12 percent in Phase III.

As Table 5.2 suggests, links related to productive activity, either looking for a job or non-email work activity, increased from 1 percent of the links before 2000 to 8 percent of the links after 2004.[5] Breaking productive activity into its two constituent parts in Table 5.3 we see that there is far more growth in the number of links related to work activity than in the number of links related to employment opportunities. After June of 2000, then, a greater proportion of the links are related to facilitating work activity (e.g., web hosting) than to facilitating job searches (e.g., online classifieds). The job opportunity links that are available are typically quite short and very general. The average

Table 5.2 Classification of Links on Yahoo! Home Page by Phase, 1996–2005

	PHASE I (10/96–6/00) (%)	PHASE II (6/00–10/04) (%)	PHASE III (11/04–12/05) (%)
Information on a hobby or interest**	25.5	16.6	10.7
Information on a specific geographic area**	18.5	14.8	6.1
Consumption—product research, travel, purchase, real estate**	7.5	11.0	13.3
Entertainment—movies, music, TV, and sports**	6.3	8.6	12.2
Yahoo! site-related information**	7.5	7.0	10.9
News**	3.6	6.0	10.0
Communication—email, IM, chat, dating sites, online groups**	3.4	4.9	8.4
Production—looking for a job or any work-related activity except email**	1.4	6.0	7.8
Health—general health, specific diseases or fitness**	4.4	2.4	2.0
Financial information	2.9	3.1	3.0
Use of a search engine**	1.7	2.2	6.3
Other**	17.2	17.5	9.7

Percentages may not equal 100% due to rounding.
Note:
** $p < 0.01$.

length of text for all links is 1.91 words, whereas the average length of text for job opportunity links is 1.58, a significant difference of about one-third of a word.[6] We can infer from this information that the Internet provides more help to individuals already employed than for those individuals looking for employment. This is problematic given the research that suggests that low-income Internet users are more likely to use the Internet to look for jobs (NTIA 2000; see also findings in Chapter 4).

A more detailed look at the kind of job postings available online gives us an even greater appreciation for the user base to which Yahoo!

Table 5.3 Work Links on Yahoo! Home Page by Phase, 1996–2005

	PHASE I (10/96–6/00) (%)	PHASE II (6/00–10/04) (%)	PHASE III (11/04–12/05) (%)
Links related to employment opportunities**	1.1	1.9	3.0
Links to facilitate any work activity except email**	0.3	4.1	4.9

Note:
** $p < 0.01$.

caters. Since 2003, Monster.com, another leading job search site, has published a monthly summary of online employment opportunities called the *Monster Employment Index*. This index is intended to measure variation and growth in online job listings.[7] The *Index* is useful because it covers all occupations, because it is repeated regularly and because the reporting categories for occupations are based on the Standard Occupational Classification System (SOC) used by the U.S. Bureau of Labor Statistics (BLS) for its regular reporting on employment trends. Figure 5.5 illustrates that there is significant growth in online employment recruitment across a full range of occupations. In occupations with the greatest increase in online employment advertisements—highlighted with the darkest shading in Figure 5.5— the number of listings more than doubled between 2003 and 2007. The great majority of these occupations are high-skilled occupations, such as management, legal, and computer occupations. Nearly all the occupations with the slowest rates of growth in online advertising— those with the lightest shading in Figure 5.5—are unskilled and semi-skilled, including production, construction, and extraction occupations.

An obvious explanation for the occupational variation in online employment listings is that those occupations with the sharpest increase in online advertising are those occupations that grew the most during this time period. Presumably there would be more listings for those occupations that were expanding most rapidly. Figure 5.6 depicts growth rates for the different occupations between 2003 and 2006, using data from the Bureau of Labor Statistics.[8] A comparison of

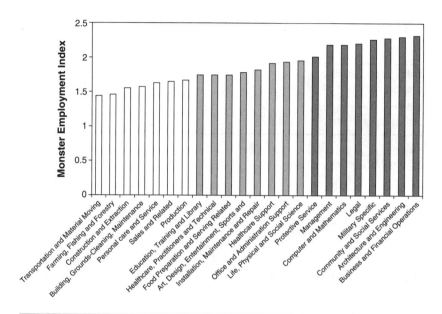

Figure 5.5 Growth in online employment advertising by occupation, 2003–2007.

Figures 5.5 and 5.6 shows that there is little relationship between growth in online advertising and growth in jobs. The shading used in Figure 5.5 is brought over to Figure 5.6 to call attention to this point. Occupations represented by lightly shaded columns saw the lowest rates of growth in online advertising. As we can see, they are not necessarily among the slowest growing occupations in Figure 5.6. For example, construction and extraction occupations had the third slowest increase in online job listing, but had the third highest rate of job growth. The weak correlation between increases in online job listings and employment growth in particular occupations can be quantified by calculating the correlation coefficient for these two measures. With a value of 1 indicating a perfect correlation and a value of 0 no relationship, the obtained value of 0.117 suggests little to no relationship.

These findings suggest that the valuable means of communication and information that define the Internet may selectively afford opportunities for some but not for others. Employment advertising, of course, is only one area in which online content caters to the privileged. What

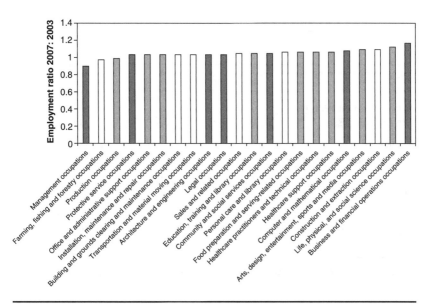

Figure 5.6 Growth in employment by occupation, 2003–2007.

about other information resources? To answer this question, we coded the sample of 18,847 Yahoo! home page links according to whether they were tied to information relevant to the same major moments we discussed in Chapter 4.[9] As we can see in Table 5.4, there were significant shifts in the number of links associated with particular moments. In Table 4.6, we saw that getting additional training and choosing a school were the only two types of decisions in which the Internet served as an information resource for at least half of all individuals with no more than a high school degree. We see in Table 5.4, however, that among all links related to major moments, the proportion related to training and education was cut approximately in half, from 25 percent in Phase I to 13 percent in Phase III. Indeed, despite the fact that "Education" started out as one of the main directory categories on Yahoo!, it has all but vanished from the home page today. In 2008, there was no regular link titled "Education" on the home page, though links to a variety of online higher education programs are routinely featured in the "Marketplace" section. Clicking on "More Yahoo! Services" in 2008 brought up a list of 61 alphabetically organized topical areas, of

Table 5.4 Links Related to Major Moments on the Yahoo! Home Page by Phase, 1996–2005

	PHASE I (10/96–6/00) (%)	PHASE II (6/00–10/04) (%)	PHASE III (11/04–12/05) (%)
Getting additional training or choosing a school	24.8	14.4	12.6
Helping self or another person with a major illness	30.0	25.1	14.3
Buying a car	13.6	16.3	18.7
Making a major investment or financial decision	18.9	17.1	18.1
Finding a new place to live	3.1	5.8	7.1
Changing jobs	9.6	21.2	29.1
Total major moment links	100.0 (456)	100.0 (881)	100.0 (182)

Percentages may not equal 100% due to rounding.
Note:
** $p < 0.01$.

which "Education" was one. At this point, the user interested in education could find a wealth of resources related to Education. But the information was buried in multiple links and was not a major feature of the website.

Let's focus our attention on one major moment in particular: the purchasing of an automobile. Whereas Table 4.5 indicates that there was little variation in vehicle purchases by education over the past two years, Table 4.6 shows that more than twice as many college graduates used the Internet to inform their purchasing decision compared with car buyers with less than a high school degree. Analyzing the text associated with the car buying links found on the sampled Yahoo! pages from 1996 through 2005 reveals that the featured vehicles tended to be more expensive makes and models during this timeframe. Clicking on Yahoo! Autos, a wealth of information is available for a total of 1,388 models. Without leaving the Yahoo! domain, users can get pricing, performance, and technical specifications, as well as read Yahoo! user reviews and ratings for vehicles they find interesting. Users may select cars by make and model, but also by seating capacity, fuel efficiency, driving performance, body style, and price. Examining the selection of vehicles by price is revealing. Over 34 percent are priced at $35,000 or higher and only 4 percent are priced at $15,000 or lower.

According to U.S. Bureau of the Census reports, the median household income in 2006 in the U.S. was $48,451 (Webster and Bishaw 2007). Data from the U.S. Bureau of Labor Statistics consumer expenditure survey indicates that the proportion of income American households spent on transportation is relatively constant, at about 20 percent across all income levels (Mittelstaedt et al. 2007). This means that at the median income level households would spend about $9,690 dollars per year on transportation. Assuming 15,000 miles a year of driving at 25 miles per gallon and a gasoline cost of $3.00 per gallon, fuel costs alone would total $9,000. With a $15,000 purchase price, a 60-month loan at 6.0 percent and a $1,000 down payment or trade-in, monthly car payments of $270.66 would add another $3,247.92 to the annual cost. As such, it is likely that the average American would spend much less than $15,000 on a car, especially since this figure does not include costs like insurance, licensing, and maintenance.

Considering more affluent households, the new vehicle information available through Yahoo! Autos is far more relevant. Using the same 20 percent assumption, a household with an income of $100,000 would have $20,000 available for transportation. In this case, even the more expensive vehicles are affordable. For example, a $45,000 luxury sedan or sport utility vehicle financed over 60 months at 6.0 percent with a $1,000 down payment, yields monthly payments of $850.64, which over 12 months combined with $9,000 for gasoline comes in at $19,208, just under the 20 percent average. Under these circumstances the wealth of information available through Yahoo! or other online resources has concrete value and meaning. Thus, as the character of online content has become increasingly commercialized, so too is it increasingly geared toward the needs and interests of the financially better-off.

If we can think of the Internet as a kind of marketplace, wherein the currency is information rather than money, we can say that the Internet rewards some users more than others. That is, some users are able to find a wealth of information on the Internet that is relevant to them and relatively easy to access. Other users will find the Internet more limited or more difficult to navigate on account that it is not structured to cater to them. Here, then, we have a system of unequal rewards. The question remains whether this system is legitimate. In addition to the individual benefits that the Internet provides select users, is there a collective benefit or social good that stems from this unequal reward system? It could certainly be argued that because some Internet users contribute more to the collective intelligence of the Internet, they should be rewarded more. In a Durkheimian sense, if they were not rewarded, they would not spend the time to share their information or communicate their ideas online. They need some incentive, and that incentive is an Internet structure that essentially caters to them and their needs. Society, in turn, benefits from the collective intelligence they provide. Our data do not answer this last question, but they do suggest that the Internet is structured in a way that benefits certain groups of users who, in turn, provide the collective intelligence for which today's Internet is well known.

Summary and Conclusion

In this chapter, we considered the division of labor, which Durkheim and other functionalists view as a hallmark of modern society. In this division of labor, each member of society fulfills particular tasks and roles, creating a system of interdependency and a sense of solidarity that effectively hold society together. Some of the roles in this division of labor are more important than others to the extent that they provide a more valuable service or make a more functional contribution to the larger society. For this, individuals that fulfill these roles reap greater rewards in the form of higher wages or salaries, greater prestige and honor, and more scarce resources. To functionalists, this form of inequality is legitimate because it serves society as a whole. This kind of perspective lends itself to examining the relationship between individuals and social structure to the extent that it highlights how social forces and social considerations act upon individuals. We do not act independently in pursuit of our own self-interests, but in coordination with other members of society for the good of the whole.

Extending the functionalist perspective to the Internet, we found that the Internet serves as a powerful window into the inner workings of society. Like society, the Internet is structured in particular ways, guiding users down certain channels of information and through particular networks of Internet links. In a Durkheimian sense, this structure is not random; it provides social order and directs individuals into their respective societal roles. Analyzing the organization and content of Yahoo!'s home page, we learned that Yahoo! has morphed over the past ten years as that structure has taken shape. Although the current number of links on the Yahoo! home page is not that different from the number in 1996, the nature of the links has changed dramatically. First, there has been a notable decline in the links that allow users to select from topically oriented directories of information. Instead, the website is designed in a way to direct users to commercial products and services. Our detailed look at employment and automobile listings revealed that these commercial links are not aimed at all web users, but rather well-to-do web users.

As the case of Yahoo! suggests, the Internet caters to a specific group of savvy Internet users. It provides information and services most relevant to them and directs them in their role as affluent consumers and producers. Structurally, the Internet rewards and benefits this group of users. But does society also benefit from this structure? Is this a case of legitimate equality? In one sense, the collective intelligence of the Internet provides a benefit to all Internet users, whether or not they use the Internet extensively or with much skill. Conducting an information search on Google.com produces a host of results based on what others found useful and relevant; looking up something on Wikipedia.com gives information provided by others; perusing Instructables.com provides access to how-to guides written by experts and amateurs the world over. One doesn't need to contribute to these sites to take advantage of them. In fact, one can limit one's use of the Internet to information consumption, rather than be among the Internet's contributing architects. One could argue, then, that Internet inequality, though it exists, matters less in the grand scheme of things. Durkheim would probably agree.

Questions for Reading, Reflection, and Debate

1 According to Durkheim, those with skills and talents are rewarded with higher salaries and prestige because society deems their roles or contributions to society more functionally important. Although this produces inequality, it is a legitimate form of inequality since society benefits from the contributions of this privileged segment of society. In this chapter, we argued that, like the market, the Internet distributes information and resources unequally, privileging some more than others. But is it the case that privileged Internet users provide important contributions to society and, hence, should be rewarded with Internet information and resources? Consider the kinds of contributions that savvy Internet users provide. Then evaluate the functional importance of these contributions with respect to society at large. Finally, discuss whether these contributions must be functionally important to justify this system of unequal rewards.

2 In this chapter, we limited our analysis to the structure of Yahoo!'s home page. There are countless other examples from the Internet that we could have used. Consider the case of Instructables.com from a functionalist perspective. What kind of division of labor do we see in this e-repository of how-to information? Are there some members of the user community who primarily produce the how-to guides available through this site? And are there others who primarily consume, or read these guides? Finally, are there non-members of this user community that might benefit from the information consumed on this site by others? Think through the relative levels of Internet savvy you would need to produce and publish these guides, as well as to browse and read these guides. Also think through the relative rewards individuals might receive for producing versus consuming these guides.

3 Functionalists focus on how social structure shapes individual action, but they tend to ignore *how* societies become structured in particular ways in the first place. As the most prominent Internet search engine, Google is structured the way it is on

account of two sets of architects: its user community and its designers. As the reader may know, a search on Google is designed to produce sponsored commercial links and unsponsored links that may or may not be commercial in nature. In the shaded area at the top of the page and again on the right side of the page, subsets of results are associated with the word "Sponsored," indicating that an organization or individual has paid to have the link prominently displayed. The remainder of the links are not paid for; they are ordered according to how popular or how many "hits" they receive by the wider community of Internet users. Google has also begun analyzing logs of past searches for each individual to tailor search results to that user's geographic area. Considering this information, weigh the extent to which Google's structure "emerges" from the coordinated actions of millions of individual users or the extent to which its structure is imposed from above by powerful commercial interests. What does this suggest about functionalism's explanatory potential?

4 Go to Wikipedia.com and look through the website for data on its history, its structure, and its usage. How might these data be used to study three concepts that are central to Durkheim's perspective: the division of labor, organic solidarity, and legitimate and illegitimate inequality? For example, what information is available concerning the process by which articles are written, published, edited, contested, and consumed? And what might this information tell us about these core concepts? In your answer, pay particular attention to the tabs under "interaction" and "toolbox," located on the left side of the web page, as well as the "discussion," "edit this page," and "history" tabs at the top of each article.

5 Consider the production and consumption sides of YouTube, the popular online video sharing site. What demographic groups are highly represented in the production and uploading of video content? What videos are most popular and what does this suggest about the users that "consume" these videos? Finally, how

has YouTube infiltrated the cultural mainstream *off* the Internet? That is, in what ways has YouTube become a cultural phenomenon in the larger society that includes Internet users and non-users?

6

INEQUALITY AND THE FUTURE
OF THE INTERNET

Of course we have no idea, now, of who or what the inhabitants of our future might be. In that sense, we have no future. Not in the sense that our grandparents had a future, or thought they did. Fully imagined cultural futures were the luxury of another day, one in which "now" was of some greater duration. For us, of course, things can change so abruptly, so violently, so profoundly, that futures like our grandparents' have insufficient "now" to stand on. We have no future because our present is too volatile . . . . We have only risk management. The spinning of the given moment's scenarios. Pattern recognition.

—*Gibson* 2003

William Gibson's 1984 science fiction novel, *Neuromancer*, popularized the term "cyberspace," which he defined as "a consensual hallucination experienced daily by billions of legitimate operators" (Gibson 1984, p. 69). The anti-hero of Gibson's novel is Case, a burned-out computer hacker who jacks in and out of the net, seeking human interaction, but finding only artificial intelligence. Some ten years before the rise of the World Wide Web, Gibson anticipated the essence of the digital age in this groundbreaking novel. And for this, he was praised as a visionary. But by the late 1990s, given the rapidity with which technological change had occurred, even Gibson was hesitant to guess what technology's future might look like. In a 1997 CNN interview he stated: "I actually feel that science fiction's best use today is the exploration of contemporary reality rather than any attempt to predict where we are going." Thus, in a recent novel, *Pattern Recognition* (2003), online chats, PowerMacs, and viral videos are the terra firma of the present, not a futuristic possibility. Gibson's new hero, Cayce (pronounced "case"), is a young marketing consultant known as a "coolhunter." Tapping into her sensitivity to patterns, she is able to predict what will be "cool" in a rapidly changing commercial culture.

To think about the Internet's future requires a bit of "coolhunting" *à la* Cayce. Lacking any real ability to predict the future, we must focus on pattern recognition to hunt down and hunt out the emerging trends in digital life. Given the evidence we've laid out in this book, we suspect that inequality will continue to be a defining feature of the Internet in years to come. As such, we'll suggest a model for understanding Internet inequality that incorporates the three perspectives outlined in this book. In presenting this integrated model, we'll show how those individuals now marginalized by digital technology may find themselves increasingly excluded from the technical skills, status markers, and content structures that are fast becoming key institutional features of the Internet age. It is in this sense that Internet inequalities may not simply endure, but intensify over time. The key to overcoming these inequalities, we suggest, is to focus on Internet *use* rather than Internet *access*. In particular, individuals must learn to use the Internet, lest they be used *by* the Internet.

To illustrate the importance of Internet use, we'll review the emerging issue of digital privacy and the ways in which an increasing segment of the user population is made vulnerable to Internet abuse. We will also explore the rising importance of virtual communities in making use of the Internet for social interaction rather than commercial profit. Privacy protection and virtual interaction are the kinds of Internet competencies that will become increasingly important in the years ahead, competencies for which we need some kind of training and skills development, as well as the motivation and interest that make these competencies relevant. We'll conclude this chapter, and this book, by questioning the limited nature of existing policy debates surrounding the Internet and by offering our own view of the Internet's future.

Exclusion and Inequality on the Internet

Early discussions of Internet inequality focused on issues of access. A key source for this discussion was a series of reports issued by the National Telecommunications and Information Administration (NTIA) beginning with their 1995 study *Falling Through the Net: A Survey of the "Have Nots" in Rural and Urban America*. This report examined variation in Internet access according to gender, race, income, education, age, and place of residence. In Chapter 2, we used similar variables to demonstrate that, with the exception of gender, these differences in access have not disappeared. And in the case of education and income, inequalities have increased. Although we confirmed the presence of an enduring "digital divide," we suggested that the language of "haves" and "have nots" limits our understanding of Internet inequality. In a country in which some form of Internet access is becoming common, we also need to examine how individuals participate in and benefit from the Internet in distinct ways. Understanding how people access the Internet, use the Internet, and benefit from the Internet is critical to understanding Internet inequalities

The three perspectives outlined in this book each suggest a window into understanding Internet inequality. In Chapter 3, for example, we outlined a conflict perspective on the Internet, demonstrating how Internet literacy has become an asset to maintain class privilege and power. As we suggested, middle-class parents inculcate their children with Internet skills and competencies that serve them well in school and the labor market. In Chapter 4, we assessed differences in digital lifestyles, as suggested by the work of Max Weber and other cultural theorists. As we demonstrated, the Internet left a much greater imprint on the lives of those with higher levels of education and income, which helps establish the Internet as a marker of at least middle-class status. Finally, in Chapter 5, we drew on the work of Emile Durkheim to outline a functionalist perspective on Internet inequality. From a functionalist perspective, the Internet rewards the well-to-do with relevant information and consumer choices. Although this reproduces inequality, it is a legitimate form of inequality to the extent that it rewards a class that is functionally important to the information economy.

Although each of these perspectives provides a different rationale for variation in Internet access, use, and savvy, all three perspectives suggest that the Internet is likely to perpetuate and perhaps even increase inequality. For conflict theory, Internet skills serve as a type of asset that allows its holders to leverage higher incomes. Hence, these skills will be passed down from parent to child in class-privileged families and will be taught in class-privileged schools. For cultural theory, Internet activities are associated with high-status groups and prestigious lifestyles. Thus, certain activities will be subject to group closure, in which low-status groups will be excluded from elite online networks and activities. And for functionalist theory, the structure of the Internet rewards privileged members of the user community with relevant information. This form of inequality represents a necessary incentive to ensure that members of the user community will lend their skills and talents to the digital world. Each perspective has a unique angle on differences in Internet use and its reverberating effects. But each approach points to inequalities that will endure even if we reach universal Internet access in this country.

Figure 6.1 depicts an integrated way of looking at Internet inequality, which incorporates all three perspectives. Here, we can see that if the cultural perspective suggests that there is an Internet-oriented lifestyle that is characteristic of individuals with high levels of education and income, we would expect that the differentiation and commercialization of online content implied by a functionalist perspective would evolve in a manner consistent with the tastes and preferences associated with this group. And if the functionalist perspective suggests that certain members of society are rewarded with valuable information and resources through the structure of Internet, we would expect these members to use this information to their income and class advantage, as the conflict perspective also holds. Finally, if the conflict perspective assumes that Internet use and competencies represent a kind of middle-class asset, we would expect that this asset would be protected by and shared among networks of privileged Internet users, as the cultural perspective describes. From the perspective of Figure 6.1, these approaches are more alike than different. It's simply that they focus on different angles of Internet

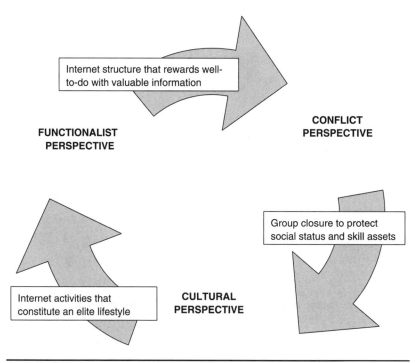

Internet structure that rewards well-to-do with valuable information

FUNCTIONALIST PERSPECTIVE

CONFLICT PERSPECTIVE

Group closure to protect social status and skill assets

Internet activities that constitute an elite lifestyle

CULTURAL PERSPECTIVE

Figure 6.1 Integrated model of Internet inequality.

privilege and functioning. In the end, poor and rich alike might have access to the Internet, but only a privileged few are able to turn to the Internet as an asset, a lifestyle, and an incentive.

Looking at Figure 6.2, we see that this integrated model is not only theoretically plausible, but empirically supported by the data presented in Chapters 3 through 5. As we see here, an Internet that is structured to provide relevant information to the well-to-do provides an incentive for certain members of society to use the Internet intensively and to develop skills in navigating the Internet. As they develop, these skills become assets, allowing individuals that possess these skills to leverage higher wages and occupational advancement. This mobility secures a place for these individuals in high-status groups, allowing them to enjoy a privileged lifestyle. Finally, as this lifestyle evolves, the Internet is restructured to more fully cater to the tastes and preferences of this

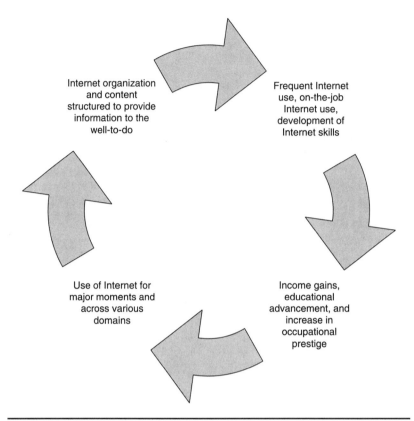

Figure 6.2 Empirical evidence supporting integrated model of Internet inequality.

well-to-do group. Thus, these forms of Internet inequality feed off one another, reproducing and even intensifying inequality over time. An integrated framework involving each of these three perspectives encourages us to view the relationship between the Internet and inequality not just as a set of variables, but as a complex process. It also helps us appreciate how this process might exacerbate inequality over time.

These findings suggest that achieving universal Internet access is not enough to end existing forms of Internet inequality. In fact, universal Internet access may do more harm than good. Without training on how to develop Internet competencies, without some mechanism to reduce forms of Internet exclusion, and without some restructuring to make Internet content more relevant, universal access is akin to allowing poor people to walk the halls of an upscale shopping mall. Not only do they lack knowledge of how to find what they're looking for, they lack a sense of belonging among the well-to-do shoppers and they lack the income that might afford them the products that are for sale in the first place. At best, the Internet's marginalized will be used *by* the Internet for the purpose of commercial profit. Thus, in addition to Internet *access*, we need to start talking about Internet *use* and Internet *structure*. Given the decentralized and unregulated nature of digital technology, the latter issue is a complex one that we do not have sufficient space to explore. Therefore, in the remaining sections of this chapter, we'll focus on the former, exploring the ways in which individuals are used by the Internet and, conversely, the ways that the Internet is used by individuals. By examining issues of digital privacy and the case of virtual communities, we'll suggest that the Internet is both a space of danger and promise. Educating individuals on how to navigate this ambiguous space is as essential as giving them access to it in the first place.

Internet (Ab)uses: The Case of Digital Privacy

One of the least talked about issues confronting Internet users today is digital privacy. Protecting personal privacy on the Internet requires a particularly savvy form of digital know-how that most users are lacking. For users and non-users alike, the development and spread of the Internet raises new and significant issues surrounding privacy. For example, the Internet sites we visit record our keystrokes and mouse clicks, as well as the personal data we enter while visiting these sites. Sites typically store "cookies" on the user's device, which allow them to gather additional information after the user leaves the site. And these are just the *legal* invasions of our privacy! Illegal activities also abound and include phishing efforts, such as advance fee email scams, often referred to as Nigerian email scams. These scams attempt to entice users to submit personal and financial information, which scam artists employ to rob users of money and identity. Holt and Graves (2007) cite one estimate that fraudulent emails scams have taken over one billion dollars from individuals and businesses between 1996 and 2006.

Though by definition non-users never enter data about themselves on the Internet, this does not protect them from digital privacy issues. Not being an Internet user does not stop www.whitepages.com from listing your phone number, address, age, the names of other members of your household, and other places you've lived. Whether you use the Internet or not, Google Maps will provide anyone an aerial photograph—and in many cases, a street-level view—of your residence. In many areas, property tax records are accessible online, as are political contributions, court rulings, building permits, and other public records. Finally, individuals may post text, photos, and videos to blogs, social networking sites and other online locations, regardless of whether the individual depicted has access to the information or even knows that it is available online.

In many cases, Internet companies are upfront about their collection and use of user data. Google, Yahoo! and other widely visited web sites, for example, routinely place a link to their "Privacy Policy" at the bottom of their home page. Few people click on these links, and much to their detriment. More often than not, these privacy policies inform users not to expect any privacy whatsoever. As an example, consider the Yahoo! privacy policy:

- Yahoo! collects personal information when you register with Yahoo!, when you use Yahoo! products or services, when you visit Yahoo! pages or the pages of certain Yahoo! partners, and when you enter promotions or sweepstakes. Yahoo! may combine information about you that we have with information we obtain from business partners or other companies.
- When you register we ask for information such as your name, email address, birth date, gender, ZIP code, occupation, industry, and personal interests. For some financial products and services we might also ask for your address, Social Security number, and information about your assets. When you register with Yahoo! and sign in to our services, you are not anonymous to us.
- Yahoo! collects information about your transactions with us and

with some of our business partners, including information about your use of financial products and services that we offer.

- Yahoo! automatically receives and records information from your computer and browser, including your IP address, Yahoo! cookie information, software and hardware attributes, and the page you request.

- Yahoo! uses information for the following general purposes: to customize the advertising and content you see, fulfill your requests for products and services, improve our services, contact you, conduct research, and provide anonymous reporting for internal and external clients.

(Yahoo! Privacy Policy, accessed on January 17, 2008)

The policy goes on to state that it will share your information with "trusted partners" for marketing purposes. Therefore, by using Yahoo!, you grant Yahoo! access to information about yourself and give Yahoo! and its advertisers tremendous power over your consumer choices and behavior.

According to Corey A. Ciocchetti, a business professor at the University of Denver, Yahoo!'s privacy policies are better than those of most Internet companies. Ciocchetti (2007) reports that in 2007, all highly visited web sites collected personal information. But only 60 percent of these sites had privacy policies that clearly explained their data collection practices. The remaining 40 percent had policy language that tended to mystify rather than clarify privacy issues. As Ciocchetti explains: "Once inside the actual privacy policy a visitor quickly encounters a vast array of legalese (e.g., 'heretofore,' 'personally identifiable information,' and 'nonaffiliated third parties') and tech-speak (e.g., 'cookie technology,' 'Web beacons,' and 'spyware/adware')" (Ciocchetti 2007, pp. 69–70). Even if clear policies are posted, most users, in their race to take advantage of the resources that brought them to the site in the first place, do not take the time to read the policies.

Like the government's ability to wiretap phone conversations of suspected terrorists, which has sparked tremendous controversy in the United States, the ability of companies on the Internet to track personal data for commercial purposes undermines some of the core values upon which the United States was founded. What is perhaps surprising is that this instance of digital eavesdropping, or e-snooping, has warranted so little concern in the broader public. Presumably, the public's indifference toward the invasion of privacy on the web is due to the lack of knowledge about most sites' privacy policies and/or confusion about what rights the individual actually has when using the Internet. But this lack of knowledge is not equally distributed across the population of Internet users. Although some individuals are particularly savvy about accessing, redacting and, when necessary, deleting information that affects their privacy, most individuals who use the Internet are not equipped to protect their privacy. For example, not all individuals are equally capable of managing the privacy settings on social networking sites like Facebook. And not everyone knows to monitor the profiles of others, where inappropriate pictures of or comments about themselves may appear. Finally, there are some who don't know that they should never put a user name and a password in the same email message, let alone a credit card number or social security number.

The issue of digital privacy is a critical one in that it is one of the more obvious ways in which everyday Internet users are used by Internet companies. Offline, of course, most of us would be hesitant to share our personal financial matters with complete strangers. And we would certainly be hesitant to share details about our shopping behavior to a stranger who appeared at our door with a clipboard of survey questions. And yet, each day, those of us who go online share quite personal information with companies eager to use this information for their own commercial gain. Protecting our privacy and managing our online presentation of self are the kind of competencies that are becoming critical in the information age. And these are the kind of Internet skills that we must inculcate in novice and experienced Internet users. Viewing the Internet as a portal into a virtual social world, rather than a book to be read in private is central to effective Internet use. As such, training individuals in Internet use as a public act rather than a private practice should be central to our policy discussion and research agenda.

Internet Uses: The Case of Virtual Communities

One of the more innovative uses of the web, one that is driven by grass-roots needs rather than commercial profit, is community organizing. And by this term, we're not referring simply to political organizing. We're talking about the construction of community relationships through the use of online technology. The issue of community has been a central one in sociology, which is motivated, in large part, by the desire to understand the social relations embedded in these communities. Ferdinand Toennies, an early German sociologist and a contemporary of Durkheim and Weber, used the German words *Gemeinshaft* and *Gesellschaft* to distinguish two fundamentally different bases for social relations. For Toennies, social relationships were grounded either in sentiment, friendship, kinship, and neighborliness (*Gemeinschaft*) or in contractual interests, rational calculation, monetary ties, and legal codes (*Gesellschaft*) (1887, 1957 translation, *Community and Society*).

Gemeinschaft and *Gesellschaft* are not empirically exclusive categories, but rather abstract representations of social arrangements that may be found existing side-by-side in a given social context. In this regard, Toennies made it clear that societies have elements of both, but to varying degrees (Cahnman 1977; Dumont 1983; Mellow 2005).[1] In general, Toennies argued, elements of *Gesellschaft* increased as societies modernized (Dumont 1983). And interpretations of Toennies argued that he was biased toward and romanticized *Gemeinschaft* (e.g., Berger 1998). Bruhn (2005), for example, claims that Toennies favored *Gemeinschaft* as the ideal type of community with its simple, intimate, private way of life, where members were bound together by common traditions, a common language, and a sense of "we-ness" (p. 30).

It is this romanticized interpretation of *Gemeinschaft* that we see echoed in Lee Siegel's book, *Against the Machine: Being Human in the Age of the Electronic Mob* (2008), which expresses deep concern over the dehumanizing effects of the information revolution. Siegel describes quite clearly the potential for information technology to create a society in which people treat one another as means and not ends:

you go online to look for something. Everyone you meet online is looking for something too. The Internet is the most deliberate, purposeful environment ever created. On the Internet an impulse is only seconds away from its gratification . . . . The criterion for judging the worth of someone you engage with online is the degree of his or her availability to your will. (Siegel 2008, p. 175)

From Siegel's perspective, the Internet is a technology used to facilitate the aims of self-serving individuals and not some idealized community of users. Like Toennie's romanticized notion of *Gemeinschaft*, Siegel looks to a pre-Internet moment for real community. The Internet age is one of self-interest, not one of mutual cooperation.

Though Toennies might have idealized *Gemeinschaft*, and bemoaned its decline with modernization, he recognized its presence even in modern communities. And this suggests a more sophisticated interpretation of the Internet and its potential for community organizing. Study after study suggests the ways in which *Gemeinschaft* endures and resurfaces in the modern age, both on- and offline. Gardner (2004), for example, examines participation in bluegrass festivals to understand "how an increasingly mobile subset of individuals grapples with courting community in a society that frequently moves, travels, relocates, or pursues leisure or lifestyle away from home" (Gardner 2004, p. 155). As the participants travel from one weekend festival to the next, they discover "spaces for intimate and inclusive *Gemeinschaft* social interaction that they find lacking in their daily lives." These are not geographically-based communities but are what Gardner calls "portable communities." Individuals belong with varying levels of commitment and the communities are made up of "loosely organized groups of similarly minded individuals who seek out one another when traveling or moving frequently from place to place" (Gardner 2004, p. 156). In short, portable communities are an inviting distraction from *Gesellschaft*-oriented routines of anonymous neighborhoods and sterile workplaces. Gardner insists that "participants in these portable communities create stable and enduring social structures that resemble 'true' neighborhoods in nearly every feature except geographic rootedness" (2004, p. 174).

Are there bluegrass-like spaces on the web, wherein users resurrect elements of *Gemeinschaft* in the otherwise fast-moving and ever-changing environment of the Internet? Evidence suggests that virtual communities are alive and well on the web. Indeed, an important side story to the commercial development of the Internet is the digital utopianism movement known as the WELL, or the Whole Earth 'Lectronic Link. Known as "the primordial ooze where the online community movement was born," the WELL first began in 1985 as a teleconferencing system (www.well.com, accessed on June 3, 1009). But it was modeled after the ideals of the *Whole Earth Catalog*, a late 1960s countercultural resource guide for cooperative, socially just, and environmentally friendly living (Turner 2006, p. 141). When the WELL brought this approach online, it gave form to what Howard Rheingold, a writer and early WELL participant, called a "virtual community" of like-minded individuals (www.rheingold.com/vc/book/index.html, accessed on June 3, 2009).

Rheingold's recognition of the potential for a sense of community to emerge online has been confirmed with the creation of thousands of such communities, typically geographically dispersed and created around a variety of niche interests. Early descriptions of online communities found them at particular virtual locations, places organized around and friendly to the community base. In the mashed-up, seamless world of Web2.0, virtual places are themselves transient. The community, thus, lies in the communication and in the information shared. For example, if someone "Diggs" something, they can communicate this information to their friends and members of their "community" without ever sharing the same virtual space. And all of this can be accessed anywhere by mobile devices. Web2.0 users are like the bluegrass festival participants—members of portable communities without a particular place on- or offline.

Access to virtual communities requires an ability to use the Internet for decidedly social purposes. One must know not simply how to access a site like Facebook, but how to use the site and how to employ mash-ups to create a seamless web of information and communication. Importantly, one must develop an online presence and identity to participate in this kind of community. Like a child, they must learn how to make friends and maintain friendships by developing and nurturing a virtual community of like-minded communicators and information seekers. The information age, what Liu (2004) describes as the "cold space of nonidentity," requires us to develop a cultural interface to interact with the virtual world (p. 76). Liu describes this as learning to be "cool." To be "cool" is to find some measure of humanity in a *Gesellschaft*-like world. But here, again, Internet *use*, in its truest sense, requires so much more than broadband and wireless access. It requires learning a new way of identifying and communicating.

Concluding Thoughts

Despite its egalitarian potential, the Internet has reinforced and, to some extent, exacerbated existing patterns of inequality. Individuals not only have different levels of Internet access, they bring different levels of skill, different motivations, and different needs to the Internet. As we've suggested throughout this chapter, they also bring varying levels of understanding about digital privacy and varying levels of "cool" to the World Wide Web. These differences combine with a particular Internet structure to privilege some Internet users over others. What we've tried to do in this book is to provide a sociological lens to map these inequalities in Internet use and structure, and to pose pointed questions about the ability of the "digital divide" debate to grapple with these matters.

Given its egalitarian *potential*, universal Internet access is a worthy goal. But as we've argued, the structure of the Internet has developed in conversation with economic and social inequalities. To "fix" Internet inequalities, then, we must tackle much more than questions of infrastructure and access. And yet this is precisely the focus of most policy discussions. In his 2007 presidential announcement speech in Springfield, Illinois, for example, Barack Obama urged Americans to "lay down broadband lines through the heart of inner cities and rural towns all across America," suggesting that Internet inequality is simply a matter of infrastructure. This view was reinforced when the new President and his team put forth a technology and innovation plan that promised, among other things, to build a modern communications infrastructure. But when we look closely at how different groups *use* the Internet, and how the Internet uses *them*, we begin to see that the story of the digital divide is not simply one of access. Therefore, DiMaggio et al. (2001) argue that lessening the digital divide requires training, in addition to infrastructure development. But because Internet technology has evolved in ways that correspond to social divides offline, even such training may provide limited redress for the kinds of inequalities that are emerging online. Without a fundamental restructuring of society, and hence a restructuring of the Internet, we may be limited in the extent to which we can make the Internet an equal opportunity structure.

Even outside possible policy interventions, we have reason to be optimistic about the future of Internet technology. As we saw with virtual communities, the development of the Internet has been driven as much by human imagination as by commercial profit. The future of the Internet does not have to be that "polar night of icy darkness" described by Weber in his anticipation of modernity; it could be a future in which inequality and innovation coexist. Indeed, we suggest a more complicated future, one foreshadowed by a now popular Web2.0 invention called "Twitter." Twitter is a microblogging service that allows users to send updates, or "tweets" to a circle of friends via short messages. Typically tweets are quick and often mundane reports of day-to-day details and on-the-spot reactions to lived experiences. Not everyone participates in Twitter. Like most Web2.0 applications, Twitter's user base is more privileged than most. But its very existence and popularity suggests something fundamentally imaginative and innovative about the Internet. These tweets and other emerging Internet-based technologies are not just more bytes in the rising tide of digital data. They are signs of a collective effort to maintain intimacy in a disenchanted world. Though our "tribes" may be nomads in the Diaspora, these communiqués serve to reassure us that we are part of something larger than the World Wide Web, a web that extends far into the horizon of a larger humanity.[2]

Questions for Reading, Reflection, and Debate

1   Among the newest forms of virtual communities are virtual
    worlds. Members of virtual worlds are represented by an avatar, a
    more or less life-like graphic representation of their body, which
    they use to navigate about 3-D space. Virtual worlds provide a
    social world in which individuals can interact with others in an
    environment beyond the physical. Visit the website for
    SecondLife (SL), the most popular virtual world
    (www.secondlife.com). Does the ability to participate in SL as an
    avatar, rather than one's "real" self, allow individuals to overcome
    the constraints of age, class, and race? Or are there ways in
    which the digitally disadvantaged are forced to contend with
    their offline status in SL? If you're curious, get a free SL account
    and see for yourself!

2   In 2008, the Pew Internet & American Life Project asked a
    panel of experts to discuss the future of the Internet. Jeff Jarvis, a
    journalism professor at the City University of New York and
    blogger for Buzzmachine.com, predicted that "We will enter a
    time of mutually assured humiliation; we [will] all live in glass
    houses. That will be positive for tolerance and understanding,
    but—even more important—I believe that young people will not
    lose touch with their friends . . . and that realization of
    permanence in relationships could—or should—lead to more
    care in those relationships." In contrast, Benjamin Ben-Baruch, a
    senior consultant and applied sociologist for Aquent, contended
    that "Privacy will become increasingly compromised and
    increasingly important. People will pay a premium for services
    that limit practicable access to so-called 'public' information
    about them . . . . Increasingly, there will be a gap between those
    who are protected from surveillance and from having private
    information exposed and those who lack privacy." Compare these
    two possible futures. Which do you think is a more likely
    outcome and why? Might these two outcomes both happen in
    the not-too-distant future?

3 When asked about children having access to the Internet in
   every classroom in America, Diane Ravitch, former U.S.
   Assistant Secretary of Labor, responded with the following: "a lot
   of politicians think if you can just put the Internet in every
   classroom kids will learn . . . . There has to be a foundation of
   knowledge so that when you turn to the Internet, you have some
   capacity for critical thought about what you see there"
   (www.edletter.org/past/issues/2001-ma/forum.shtml). Now
   consider the "One Laptop per Child" initiative
   (http://laptop.org/en), which seeks to put low-cost laptops into
   the hands of poor children. What might Ravitch say about this
   initiative and its ability to educate hundreds of thousands of
   under-privileged children around the world? What is your
   opinion of this initiative? Given what you've learned in this
   book, what kind of training would you add to this initiative such
   that these children might learn how to use the Internet in
   beneficial ways?

NOTES

Chapter 1: A Sociology of the Internet

1 Information retrieved on June 1, 2009 from: www.oecd.org/document/23/ 0,3343,en_2649_34225_33987543_1_1_1_1,00.html.
2 The Internet Society was created in 1992 to support the technical evolution of the Internet; to educate regarding the technology, use, and application of the Internet; to promote the Internet for the benefit of educational institutions, industry, and society at large; and to provide a forum for the development of new Internet technologies and applications (www.isoc.org).
3 Internet protocols are the rules for packaging and addressing data in a network environment. Unlike telephone connections, which rely on establishing and maintaining a circuit, the Internet relies on a connectionless network—one that allows for communication even if the circuit is broken.
4 For the technically inclined, RFC numbers are provided and readers can consult the primary sources in the RFC repository, maintained by the IETF Secretariat at www.ietf.org/rfc.html.
5 In 1992, the current organizational structure of the Internet was formed with the creation of the Internet Society, which provided a coordinating body to manage the Internet's evolution.
6 Cybercash Inc. went bankrupt in 2001, but its operating assets were bought by a group that included VeriSign, a current leader in online payment systems.

Chapter 2: Internet Use Among American Adults

1 These age patterns may lead us to conclude that the proportion of American Internet users will continue to increase as the oldest cohort passes away and is replaced by younger cohorts who are more likely to use the Internet. But there may be an interesting measurement twist to this story. Today's teens tend to rely more heavily on cell phones, gaming consoles, and other "information appliances" than today's young adults (Zittrain 2008). Although many of these devices are tied to the Internet (e.g.

Blackberries), individuals may not equate using these devises with using the Internet, reporting lower levels of Internet use as a result.

2   Results for individuals employed part-time are not shown but are virtually identical to those for individuals employed full-time.

3   The Pew Project does not collect data on all activities with every survey. Thus, Table 2.4 is a compilation of results from a number of surveys. The date of interview is provided for each activity.

4   Again, the Pew Project does not collect data on all activities with every survey. Like Table 2.4, Table 2.5 is a compilation of results from a number of surveys. The dates of interview are provided for each activity. A yearly rate of change is provided in the final column to facilitate comparisons across activities since the time elapsed between observations varies with each activity.

5   Production here is defined as the creation of goods or services. Consumption would include the use of such goods and services.

6   Of course using the Internet *at* work does not necessarily mean that one is using the Internet *for* work. For example, vacation planning, newspaper reading, and any number of other activities routinely take place online at work even though these are not work-related. Even so, respondents who indicate that they use the Internet at work probably use the Internet *for* work at least some of the time.

Chapter 3: Internet Inequality from a Conflict Perspective

1   We are skirting a critical point made by Wright here, namely that these skills should have some credential attached to them to be of real value in the labor market.

2   See www.umass.edu/preferen/gintis/soced.pdf, accessed on June 22, 2009.

3   On-the-job Internet use is particularly important here because we are conceptualizing Internet use as a skill that confers some market advantage. To have a market advantage, Internet use must be related to one's occupation or job, rather than one's recreational pursuits. Although it is certainly the case that an individual might use the Internet at work for recreational purposes (e.g., ordering flowers online for Mother's Day), we'll assume here that the bulk of on-the-job Internet use is job-related. In doing so, we follow earlier studies (e.g., Krueger 1993) that consider on-the-job computer use as a measure of technical skills that have the potential to enhance individual earnings.

4   These results do not separate out those who were interviewed on a Sunday or Monday and were less likely to have been at work on the previous day. This may lead to a minor underestimation of the percentage of those who went online at work, particularly in 2000. By 2005, as is noted in Table 3.2, employed individuals were just as likely to go online on the weekend as during the work week, but we are unable to know to what extent their weekend online activities were work-related.

5   Family income is only an indirect measure of individual earnings. If individual earnings were available in the Pew data, the observed relationship would likely be stronger.

6   Although these are different data sources, the data are relatively comparable. For example, 41 percent of all Pew respondents and 42 percent of all CPS respondents said they used the Internet at work. Likewise, CPS found that 64 percent of professional and related occupations used the Internet at work; the comparable estimate in the Pew data is 65 percent.

7   Pew used the following occupational categories: professional worker (lawyer, doctor, teacher, etc.); manager, executive, or official (store manager, business executive,

government official, etc.); business owner (any business owner with two or more employees); clerical or office worker (typist, receptionist, bank teller, etc.); sales worker (store clerk, telemarketer, etc.); manufacturer's representative (sales representative); service worker (waiter, hairstylist, policeman, etc.); skilled trade or craft (electrician, baker, plumber, etc.); semi-skilled worker (machine operator, assembly line worker, truck driver, etc.); laborer (construction worker, dock worker, garbage man, etc.).

8 To truly get to the type of capital that Wright talks about would require data on technical certification that is acquired independent of a college degree—for example, a Microsoft Certified IT Professional (MCITP), a Cisco Certified Internetwork Expert (CCIE), or a Red Hat Certified Engineer (RHCE). Data from a Pew survey of over 7,000 IT professionals indicate that these certifications do, indeed, lead to significantly higher incomes independent of education and work experience (Chevalier 2008).

Chapter 4: Internet Inequality from a Cultural Perspective

1 Weber actually distinguishes between three dimensions of power: class, status, and party. The third, party, is understood by Weber as the primary means of collective agency for class and status groups. In this chapter, we restrict the discussion to *individual* characteristics associated with Weber's notion of power, namely class and status.

2 The odds ratios presented in Table 4.1 should be interpreted as follows. Significant values greater than one indicate increased odds of having gone online and significant values less than one indicate decreased odds. A magnitude greater than one represents the percentage increase in the odds. If you subtract the magnitude less than one from one, you have the percentage decrease in the odds. For example, the odds ratio of 1.12 for women-to-men Internet use on the day prior in Model [1] means that women are 12 percent more likely to have gone online the previous day than men. The odds ratio of 0.47 for black-to-white and others indicates that blacks are 53 percent less likely to have gone online than whites and others.

3 The GSS did not ask questions about Internet use on the day prior to interview, thus we do not have a good measure of daily Internet use in this case.

4 The 2004 GSS included measures of both individual and family income. We'll use the latter as a proxy for social class since this provides some degree of comparability with the Pew data, which were used in Table 4.1. As well, family income captures the overall class situation of individuals who are not currently earning their own income, but who enjoy certain class resources on account of the income provided by other family members.

5 The reader might have had similar questions with regard to Figure 4.3. Some of the difference in parents' education between Internet users and non-users is due to the latter being older and having parents of a generation that, on average, had less education. Model [2] in Table 4.4, however, illustrates that this does not explain the full effect.

6 Cutting the sample size has the effect of increasing the standard error for a given amount of variation. Thus, a similar observed relationship may no longer be statistically significant.

7 Conversely, the Pew data set, which *does* allow us to construct online activity footprints, does *not* contain occupational measures.

8 Unlike Figures 4.5 and 4.6, in which online activities were organized around two major axes (information–communication and production–consumption), there is no particular logic to the organization of online activities in Figure 4.7. Because the

ordering of activities is the same in each graph, however, the comparison of footprints between levels of education is meaningful.

9 Again, if a variable has no effect, the estimated odds ratio will be 1.0, meaning that the odds are even. A number greater than one means that increasing the value of the independent variable will increase the odds of one outcome relative to the other; a number less than one indicates that such a change in the independent variable will decrease the odds. For example, an odds ratio of 1.20 would indicate a 20 percent increase in the odds. With numbers less than 1.0 the percentage change is obtained by subtracting the odds ratio from 1.0. For example an odds ratio of 0.80 indicates a 20 percent decrease in the odds.

10 The interpretation of the odds ratios for educational achievement and household income are slightly different. Age is a continuous variable ranging, in this case, from 18 to 93 years old. Rather than measuring education in years and family income in dollars, we created categories—a range of years in the case of education, and a range of dollars in the case of income. These categories are "ordinal" such that they are ordered from least to greatest. But the language, "a one-unit change" in the independent variable no longer makes sense. In such cases, we choose one category for each variable as a reference group and estimate odds ratios for the effect of being in each of the other categories relative to the reference group.

11 Here, the analysis is restricted to adults 25 years of age and older. Not only is use highest among this age group, but those younger than 25 are unlikely to have finished their education. Level of education is, therefore, more meaningful for those 25 years and older.

Chapter 5: Internet Inequality from a Functionalist Perspective

1 Rounding out the top ten, in order: Google, YouTube, Windows Live, MSN, MySpace, Wikipedia, Facebook, Blogger.com, and Yahoo!Japan (www.alexa.com/site/ds/top_sites?ts_mode=global&lang=none, accessed May 19, 2008).

2 The Yahoos were characters in Jonathan Swift's *Gulliver's Travels*, who were obsessed with finding a particular type of shining stones:

> "That in some fields of his country there are certain shining stones of several colors, whereof the Yahoos are violently fond, and when part of these stones are fixed in the earth, as it sometimes happeneth, they will dig with their claws for whole days to get them out, carry them away, and hide them by heaps in their kennels" (Swift et al. 2007, p. 249).

This provides an interesting metaphor for an Internet search.

3 It is true that the user may blaze his or her own trail through the Internet, most often by using a search engine. Indeed, a search engine has held a prominent position on the Yahoo! home page throughout this time period. But like portal pages, Internet searches have their own logic and, some would say, their own politics.

4 Efforts to obtain historical "click-through" data on specific links from Yahoo! were unsuccessful.

5 Detailed job listings became an increasingly important part of Yahoo! after the portal acquired the online recruiting service, HotJobs, in February of 2002. At the time, Media Metrix rated HotJobs.com as the leading job search site and among the top 50 visited web sites of any type. In November of 2002, the technical integration of

HotJobs and Yahoo! Careers was complete and links to their combined employment search resources became a regular feature on the Yahoo! home page.

6 Though one-third of a word may not sound like much in this case, comparing the two means yields a T-value of 12.48, meaning that a difference this large would happen with a probability of less than 1 in 10,000 due to chance.

7 According to Kathryn Burns of Monsterworldwide.com, "The baseline of the Index (100) represents the average online job availability of the first 12 months of data that was culled from a large, representative selection of corporate career sites and job boards, including Monster, from September 2003–October 2004" (Personal correspondence, December 5, 2007).

8 BLS data for 2007 were not yet available. All BLS data are based on publicly available data from the Occupational Employment Statistics program www.bls.gov/oes.

9 Two pairs of categories were merged for this purpose. Getting additional training was combined with choosing a school or college, and helping another person with a major illness was combined with dealing yourself with a major illness. This gives us six rather than eight categories for major life moments, which are listed in Table 5.4.

Chapter 6: Inequality and the Future of the Internet

1 In this respect, *Gemeinschaft* and *Gesellschaft* are different from Durkheim's notion of mechanical and organic solidarity. Durkheim described a development process, whereby mechanical solidarity gave way to organic solidarity in the process of modernization.

2 Here, too, is another example of the pace of change in Internet technology and use. While some readers may not be familiar with Twitter, the number has undoubtedly shrunk since I first described this question. The first draft of this chapter was written in April of 2007, about the same time that Barack Obama began to use Twitter as part of his Presidential campaign and nearly two years before Ashton Kutcher challenged CNN to see who could be the first Twitter user to have a million followers. In two short years, Twitter has gone from cool to a media commodity. The trick for an Internet coolhunter will be to find what is tomorrow's equivalent of yesterday's Twitter.

BIBLIOGRAPHY

Abel, Thomas and William C. Cockerham. 1993. "Lifestyle or Lebensfuehrung? Critical Remarks on the Mistranslation of Weber's 'Class, Status, Party'." *Sociological Quarterly* 34: 551–6.

Agre, Philip F. 2002. "Cyberspace as American Culture." *Science as Culture* 11: 171–89.

Althusser, Louis. 1971. *Lenin and Philosophy*. New York, NY: Monthly Review Press.

Berger, Bennett M. 1998. "Disenchanting the Concept of Community." *Society* 35(2): 324–7.

Bimber, Bruce. 2000. "The Gender Gap on the Internet." *Social Science Quarterly* 81: 868–76.

Bolt, D. and R. Crawford. 2000. *Digital Divide: Computers and Our Children's Future*. New York, NY: TV Books.

Bonfadelli, Heinz. 2002. "The Internet and Knowledge Gaps: A Theoretical and Empirical Investigation." *European Journal of Communication* 17: 65–84.

Bourdieu, Pierre. 1986. "The Forms of Capital." In *Handbook of Theory and Research for the Sociology of Education*, edited by J. Richardson. New York, NY: Greenwood.

Bourdieu, Pierre and Jean-Claude Passeron. 1977. *Reproduction in Education, Society, and Culture*. Beverly Hills, CA: Sage Publications.

Bowles, Samuel and Herbert Gintis. 1976. *Schooling in Capitalist America: Educational Reform and the Contradictions of Economic Life*. New York, NY: Basic Books.

——. 2002. "Schooling in Capitalist America Revisited." *Sociology of Education* 75: 1–18.

Broom, Leonard and Robert G. Cushing. 1977. "A Modest Test of an Immodest Theory: The Functional Theory of Stratification." *American Sociological Review* 42: 157–69.

Bruhn, John G. 2005. *The Sociology of Community Connections*. New York, NY: Springer.

Buckley, Walter. 1958. "Social Stratification and the Functional Theory of Social Differentiation." *American Sociological Review* 23: 369–75.

——. 1963. "On Equitable Inequality." *American Sociological Review* 28: 799–801.

Bureau of Labor Statistics. 2005. *Computer and Internet Use at Work in 2003*. Washington, DC: United States Department of Labor.

Cahnman, Werner J. 1977. "Toennies in America." *History and Theory* 16: 147–67.

Card, David and John DiNardo. 2002. "Skill-Biased Technological Change and Rising Wage Inequality: Some Problems and Puzzles." *Journal of Labor Economics* 20(4): 733–83.

Chevalier, Michael. 2008. *2008 IT Skills and Salary Report: A Joint Study by TechRepublic and Global Knowledge*. Louisville, KY: CNET Networks.

Ciocchetti, Corey A. 2007. "E-Commerce and Information Privacy: Privacy Policies as Personal Information Protectors." *American Business Law Journal* 44(1): 55–126.

Dahrendorf, Ralf. 1967. *Society and Democracy in Germany*. Garden City, NY: Anchor.

Davis, Kinsley and Wilbert Moore. 1945. "Some Principles of Stratification." *American Sociological Review* 10: 242–9.

Davis, Kingsley, Marion J. Levy Jr. and Walter Buckley. 1959. "Communications: Stratification and Functionalism: An Exchange." *American Sociological Review* 24: 82–6.

DiMaggio, Paul. 1987. "Classification in Art." *American Sociological Review* 52: 440–55.

DiMaggio, Paul, Eszter Hargittai, W. Russell Numan and John P. Robinson. 2001. "Social Implications of the Internet." *Annual Review of Sociology* 27: 307–36.

Dumont, Louis. 1983. "Interaction Between Cultures: Herder's Volk and Fichte's Nation." In *Ethnicity, Identity and History: Essays in Memory of Werner J. Cahman*, edited by Joseph B. Maier and Chaim I. Waxman. Transaction, pp. 13–26.

Durkheim, Emile. 1933. *The Division of Labor in Society*. New York, NY: The Free Press.

——. 1938 [1895]. *The Rules of Sociological Method*. 8th ed. Translated by Sarah A. Solovay and John M. Mueller, edited by George E. G. Catlin. Chicago, IL: The University of Chicago Press.

Dvorak, Phred. 2009. "On the Street and On Facebook: The Homeless Stay Wired." *The Wall Street Journal*, May 30. Retrieved July 2, 2009 (http://online.wsj.com/article/SB124363359881267523.html).

Erickson, Bonnie H. 1996. "Culture, Class, and Connections." *American Journal of Sociology* 102: 217–52.

Fox, Susannah and Gretchen Livingston. 2007. *Hispanics with Lower Levels of Education and English Proficiency Remain Largely Disconnected from the Internet*. (Figure 1. Internet Use Among Hispanics, Whites, and Blacks). Washington, DC: Pew Hispanic Center and Pew Internet Project.

Gardner, Robert Owen. 2004. "The Portable Community: Mobility and Modernization in Bluegrass Festival Life." *Symbolic Interaction* 27: 155–78.

Gibson, William. 1984. *Neuromancer*. New York, NY: Ace Book.

——. 2003. *Pattern Recognition*. New York, NY: Penguin Group.

Giroux, Henry A. 1983. *Theory and Resistance in Education: A Pedagogy for the Opposition*. Amherst, MA: Bergin & Garvey.

Hargittai, Eszter. 2002. "Beyond Logs and Surveys: In-Depth Measures of People's Web Use Skills." *Journal of the American Society for Information Science & Technology* 53: 1239–44.

——. 2006. "Hurdles to Information Seeking: Spelling and Typographical Mistakes During Users' Online Behavior." *Journal of the Association of Information Systems*.

Himmelweit, Susan. 1991. "Reproduction and the Materialist Conception of History: A Feminist Critique." In *The Cambridge Companion to Marx*, edited by Terrell Carter. Cambridge: Cambridge University Press.

Hoffman, Donna L. and Thomas P. Novak. 1998. "Bridging the Racial Divide on the Internet." *Science*, April 17: 390–1.

Hogan, Richard. 2005. "Was Wright Wrong? High-Class Jobs and the Professional Earnings Advantage." *Social Science Quarterly* 86: 645–63.

Holt, Thomas J. and Danielle C. Graves. 2007. "A Qualitative Analysis of Advanced Fee Fraud Schemes." *The International Journal of Cyber-Criminology* 1: 137–54.

Horrigan, John and Lee Rainie. 2006. *The Internet's Growing Role in Life's Major Moments.* Washington, DC: Pew Internet & American Life Project. Retrieved July 1, 2009 (www.pewinternet.org/~/media//Files/Reports/2006/PIP_Major%20Moments_2006.pdf.pdf).

Huaco, George A. 1963. "A Logical Analysis of the Davis and Moore Theory of Stratification." *American Sociological Review* 28: 801–4.

Johnson, Steven. 2006. *The Ghost Map: The Story of London's Most Terrifying Epidemic—and How it Changed Science, Cities, and the Modern World.* New York, NY: Riverhead Books.

Kling, Rob. 1998. "Technological and Social Access on Computing, Information and Communication Technologies." White Paper for Presidential Advisory Committee on High-Performance Computing and Communications, Information Technology, and the Next Generation Internet.

Krol, Ed. 1992. *The Whole Internet User's Guide and Catalog.* Sebastopol, CA: O'Reilly and Associates Inc.

Krueger, Alan B. 1993. "How Computers Have Changed The Wage Structure: Evidence From Micro Data." *Quarterly Journal of Economics* 108: 33–60.

Levy, Frank and Richard Murnane. 2004. *The New Division of Labor: How Computers are Creating the Next Job Market.* Princeton, NJ: Princeton University Press.

Liu, Alan. 2004. *The Laws of Cool: Knowledge Work and the Culture of Information.* Chicago, IL: University of Chicago Press.

MacLeod, Jay. 1995. *Ain't No Making It: Aspirations and Attainment in a Low-Income Neighborhood.* Boulder, CO: Westview Press.

Mark, Noah. 2003. "Culture and Competition: Homophily and Distancing Explanations for Cultural Niches." *American Sociological Review* 68: 319–45.

Marx, Karl. 1978 [1848]. *Wage Labor and Capital.* In *The Marx-Engels Reader*, edited by Robert C. Tucker. 2nd ed. New York, NY: W.W. Norton Company.

——. 1978 [1867]. *Capital Volume One.* In *The Marx-Engels Reader*, edited by Robert C. Tucker. 2nd ed. New York, NY: W.W. Norton Company.

Marx, Karl and Friedrich Engels. 1978 [1848]. *The Communist Manifesto.* In *The Marx-Engels Reader*, edited by Robert C. Tucker. 2nd ed. New York, NY: W.W. Norton Company.

Mellow, Muriel. 2005. "The Work of Rural Professionals: Doing the Gemeinschaft-Gesellschaft Gavotte." *Rural Sociology* 70: 50–69.

Miron, L. F. 1996. *The Social Construction of Urban Schooling: Situating the Crisis.* Cresskill, NJ: Hampton Press.

Mittelstaedt, John D., James C. Witte, Robert Hoopes and Jeffrey Weiss. 2007. "Asset-Limited, Income-Constrained Consumers: A Macromarketing Perspective." In *Macromarketing and Development: Building Bridges and Forging Alliances,* edited by Stacey Menzel Baker and Daniel Westbrook. Washington, DC: International Society for Marketing and Development and the Macromarketing Society.

Nakao, Keiko and Judith Treas. 1990. "Computing 1989 Occupational Prestige Scores," GSS Methodological Report No. 70. Chicago, IL: NORC.

Nakao, Keiko, Robert W. Hodge and Judith Treas. 1990. "On Revising Prestige Scores for All Occupations," GSS Methodological Report No. 69. Chicago, IL: NORC.

NTIA (National Telecommunications and Information Administration). 1995. *Falling Through the Net: A Survey of the "Have Nots" in Rural and Urban America.* July. Washington, DC: U.S. Department of Commerce.

NTIA. 1998. *Falling Through the Net II: New Data on the Digital Divide*. July. Washington, DC: U.S. Department of Commerce.

——. 1999. *Falling Through the Net: Defining the Digital Divide*. November. Washington, DC: U.S. Department of Commerce.

——. 2000. *Falling Through the Net: Toward Digital Inclusion*. October. Washington, DC: U.S. Department of Commerce.

——. 2002. *A Nation Online: How Americans Are Expanding their Use of the Internet*. February. Washington, DC: U.S. Department of Commerce.

Parsons, Talcott. 1940. "An Analytical Approach to the Theory of Social Stratification." *The American Journal of Sociology* 45(6): 841–62.

Pew Internet & American Life Project. 2000. "The Internet Life Report." Washington, D.C. Accessed on October 20th 2009 (http://www.pewinternet.org/~/media//Files/Reports/2000/Report1.pdf.pdf).

Poggi, Gianfranco. 2000. *Durkheim*. Oxford: Oxford University Press.

Rainie, Lee and Bill Tancer. 2007. Data Memo. Washington, DC: Pew Internet & American Life Project. Retrieved August 2, 2009 (www.pewinternet.org/~/media//Files/Reports/2007/PIP_Wikipedia07.pdf).

Sawyer, R. Keith. 2002. "Durkheim's Dilemma: Toward a Sociology of Emergence." *Sociological Theory* 20: 227–47.

Siegel, Lee. 2008. *Against the Machine: Being Human in the Age of the Electronic Mob*. New York, NY: Random House.

Spooner, Tom and Lee Rainey. 2000. *African-Americans and the Internet*. Washington, DC: Pew Internet & American Life Project.

Stinchcombe, Arthur L. 1963. "Some Empirical Consequences of the Davis-Moore Theory of Stratification." *American Sociological Review* 28(5): 805–8.

——. 1983. *Economic Sociology*. New York, NY: Academic Press.

Strover, S. 1999. *Rural Internet Connectivity*. Columbia, MO: Rural Policy Research Institute.

Swift, Jonathan, Scott McKowen, and Arthur Pober. 2007. *Gulliver's Travels*. New York, NY: Sterling Publishing Company.

Toennies, Ferdinand. 1957 [1887]. *Community and Society*. East Lansing, MI: The Michigan State University Press.

Tumin, Melvin M. 1953. "Some Principles of Stratification: A Critical Analysis." *American Sociological Review* 18: 387–93.

Turner, Fred. 2006. *From Counterculture to Cyberculture: Stewart Brand, the Whole Earth Network and the Rise of Digital Utopianism*. Chicago, IL: The University of Chicago Press.

U.S. Census Bureau, Current Population Survey, November 2007. Internet release date: June 2009.

U.S. Bureau of Labor Statistics Office of Occupational Statistics and Employment Projections. *Occupational Outlook Handbook. 2008–2009 Edition*.

U.S. Department of Education, National Center for Education Statistics, Fast Response Survey System (FRSS), *Internet Access in U.S. Public Schools and Classrooms: 1994–2005 – Table 413*, prepared July 2007.

UN (United Nations). 1999. *Human Development Report*. New York, NY: Oxford University Press.

Weber, Max. 1946. *From Max Weber*. Translated by H. H. Garth and C. Wright Mills. New York, NY: Oxford University Press.

——. 1947. *The Theory of Social and Economic Organizations*, edited by Talcott Parsons. New York, NY: The Free Press.

Webster, Bruce H., Jr. and Alemayehu Bishaw. 2007. U.S. Census Bureau, American
    Community Survey Reports, ACS-08, *Income, Earnings, and Poverty Data from the
    2006 American Community Survey*. Washington, DC: U.S. Government Printing
    Office.
Wesolowski, Wlodzimierz. 1962. "Some Notes on the Functional Theory of
    Stratification." *Polish Sociological Bulletin* 5–6: 28–38.
Willis, Paul. 1977. *Learning to Labor: How Working Class Kids Get Working Class Jobs*. New
    York, NY: Columbia University Press.
Wright, Erik Olin. 1979. *Class Structure and Income Determination*. New York, NY:
    Academic Press.
——. 1985. *Classes*. London: Verso.
——. 1997. *Class Counts: Comparative Studies in Class Analysis*. Cambridge: Cambridge
    University Press.
Zittrain, Jonathan. 2008. *The Future of the Internet and How to Stop It*. New Haven, CT:
    Yale University Press.

INDEX

Note: *italic* page numbers denote references to figures/tables.

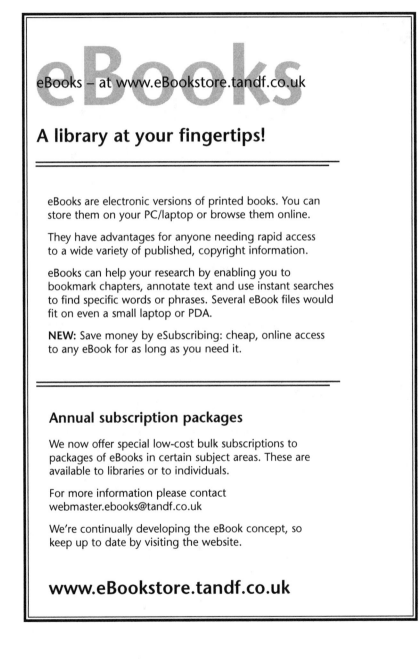